# Break Through
## Featuring
# Nikki Sheppard

# Break Through Featuring Nikki Sheppard

Powerful Stories
from Global Authorities
That Are Guaranteed
to Equip Anyone for
Real Life Breakthrough

Nikki Sheppard

Johnny Wimbrey

Nik Halik

Les Brown

and other leading authorities

WIMBREY TRAINING SYSTEMS
SOUTHLAKE, TEXAS

# ARE YOU AN OVERCOMER?

Do you have a story to tell and want to share your journey of overcoming challenges and adversities to experiencing a break through that changed your life? If so, please go to our website:
**www.CoStarAuthor.com**

Complete the online application. We have representatives on standby right now to interview you.
**www.CoStarAuthor.com**

**It's about time! People could be reading about you!**

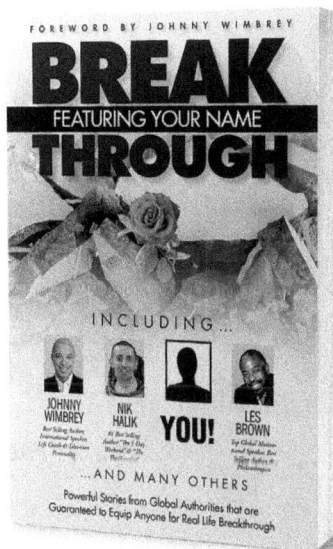

# Table of Contents

# Foreword

Think back to the hardest, darkest times in your life. What were you going through? How many times did you fail? How did you break through the difficulties and barriers you faced? How did you finally reach the success you knew you deserved?

Why do I ask this? Why do I care about the bad times and failures in your life? I care because how you handled the bad times tell me what type of person you are. I care because the choices you make when you face failure and the lessons you learn as you break through define you.

I can feel your skepticism. You think, really? Failure's important? Why?

Well, I know this to be true. I have had failures and troubles, and my choices turned me into the man I am today. I managed to break past and break through those times.

This is true, too, with the amazing group of authors I have asked to join me in *Break Through*.

I am honored to be joined by the men and women who have made deliberate sacrifices to contribute chapters to this book. Les Brown, Nik Halik, and every one of our other authors will inspire you with their stories of how they broke through their failures and barriers.

All had pain, rejection, and setbacks, and all were able to assess where they were and to make the necessary choices. Every author honestly shares their mistakes and successes with us.

Our *Break Through* authors are brave and fascinating, full of faith in their futures, and generous with their truths. They will help you navigate the crossroads you encounter and help you make sure your choices send you down the path of empowerment, confidence, and success. I am confident they will help you on your journey.

I introduce you now to my *Break Through* partners. Each one is someone I am proud to call a co-author and friend.

—**Johnny Wimbrey**

# CHAPTER ONE

# Inspect
# What You Expect

## Johnny Wimbrey

There are many things upon which I am not an authority, and there are many areas in which I will never be able to claim to be an expert, but I can tell you with total confidence that I *am* the authority on the expectation of success.

Every day, I wake up with the expectation for another level of success. I *expect* to find success mentally, emotionally, spiritually, financially, with love, with compassion, and with sensitivity.

I know I will have more of everything that matters to me, and it's just not material things. I crave and expect more knowledge, more honesty, and more good people in my life. My expectation is not arrogant, it's not greedy. My expectation is an intrinsic part of me, and I have honed it and practiced it since I was eighteen years old.

I am Johnny Wimbrey. I am a public speaker and entrepreneur, known around the world for inspiring people and helping them to change their lives. I have built a wonderful life with my wife and children. Now I'm in the privileged position of being able to give back to my community and around the globe.

No one, myself included, would have expected this—let alone predicted it—based on who I used to be. The choices I made, however, made me the man I am today.

Rejection framed my young life. My earliest memory is being hungry in a shelter for battered women. I was three years old and wanted some milk that I found when I opened the refrigerator door. Someone slammed the door on my fingers and told me the refrigerator wasn't ours and the milk wasn't mine to drink because it belonged to another family at the shelter.

That was probably the moment I grasped the unhappy facts: Yes, my mother had left my abusive, alcoholic father; we were temporary guests in a battered women's shelter; my two older brothers and I were homeless.

That feeling of rejection became the mainstay of my childhood and adolescence. My brothers, mother, and I had fled from Texas to California and I didn't see my father for years. I thought he rejected us.

My mother sent us back to live with him a few years later, and I didn't see her for the next three years of my life. More rejection. It was better to think she was dead than she had rejected us. I spent my elementary school years with my unpredictable, alcoholic father who was always busy, doing my best to keep up with my two big brothers: one a future felon, the other a future minister.

I didn't ask to move to California; I didn't ask to be sent back away from my mother, I definitely didn't ask to live with my father again. Looking back, though, I'm so glad I did live with him during those formative years. He gave me the basis for my understanding of expectation.

My father worked as a trash collector for the city. He didn't work in our poor neighborhood; his route took him over to the other side of town, the *rich* side of town. Every year when we had the long Christmas school holiday, my dad took us three boys along after work.

My father wanted us to see what else was out there in the world. He wanted us to see all the things we could have. He pushed us to open our eyes to the innumerable possibilities we had in front of us. Those trips taught me to despise the word *average*. My father raised my expectations. Not then, but later in my adolescence, I took it upon myself to rise to the challenge.

My own expectation for daily increase comes from a garbage man who refused to allow me to accept "average." He taught me to train my vision.

It took me a while to perfect this vision. It was focused on the wrong things in high school, when I made some of the worse decisions of my life. Unfortunately, my focus involved cigarettes, alcohol, drugs, and guns. My teachers told me they saw potential and talent in me and I ignored them. Who were they to tell me how to run my life? I was barreling down a one-way path headed to gang violence, substance abuse, prison, and a literal dead end.

When I was eighteen years old and a junior in high school, my path took a sudden turn when my good friend Mookie was killed by a rival. I went to Mookie's wake to say goodbye, and my brain was teeming with thoughts of death, grief, anger, and vengeance. I packed my gun as I got dressed that evening. I was looking for revenge, ready for a fight, with no glimmer of consequences or the future in my thoughts.

Brooding in my pew, I was barely listening to the speakers until Mookie's mother got up. I knew her, so I gave her the courtesy of listening to her fully. She talked with grace about my dear friend, her son, expressing not only her pain for his loss but actual forgiveness. She stood in front of Mookie's friends, family, and community and forgave her son's murderer. There was no room for interpretation:

"I forgive the man who shot my son."

She could have easily given in to her own anger and thoughts of revenge. She could have lashed out at those who loved her or withdrawn from her life altogether. But she didn't. If Mookie's *own mother*, the woman who loved him more than anyone else on this earth did, could forgive, what right did *I* have to seek vengeance?

A switch went on in my brain. I *knew* this moment was going to change my life. I knew my sudden awareness came straight from God. I was sitting there, conscious and aware, and I heard it clearly, just as if He had leaned over and whispered it directly into my ear: *This will change your life.*

I didn't hear Him because I was better or smarter than everyone around me; I was just ready to listen. God's message was flowing over everyone who was sitting with me; I was tuned to "receive."

I leaned forward and looked up and down the pew. My friends were radiating energy and anger. I could almost see the waves of vengeance coming off their bodies. Two seconds earlier, I was just like them. No more. The moment I changed, sitting there in the pew at Mookie's wake, I knew I expected more than I had the moment before.

My body stilled and I started breathing deeply. If I could have seen into the future, I would have known that every one of Mookie's and my friends would get long-term prison sentences. Perhaps I already did know this.

I knew we had been headed down the same path to the

same dead end. I knew I could have more than this. *I could be more than this.*

After everyone said their "peace" and we were milling around outside, I pulled Reverend Fitzgerald aside.

"Can I talk to you for a second?"

"Of course, son. What is it?"

"I want to give you my gun. If I give you my gun, I know I won't do anything crazy. Reverend, please take it. I don't want to live like this anymore. I am serious this time."

"You know if you give this to me, I'm not going to give it back."

"Yes, sir."

That was it. I gave him my gun. I stopped selling drugs. I stopped breaking the law. I just stopped. The next day I met Crystal, who became my wife a few years later.

I walked away from the life I had been leading. I said I was changing. And I did.

I was blessed with the chance to take what I had been given and use it to climb up and out. My prayers, my conversations with God, and the knowledge that He would give me what I needed when I needed it most, helped me every step of the way. My accomplishments didn't just belong to me; I knew I was being watched and constantly assisted. Instead of giving me complacency, my knowledge that I was never completely alone gave me both comfort and the confidence I needed to take matters into my own hands.

I began to inspect, what I expect.

It saddens me that people feel guilty for expecting more. Why is this the case? Why do they feel uncomfortable if they *expect* more success? Why do they dial back on that verb and replace it with a less aggressive one like "hope?"

The meaning completely changes when you *hope* for more success, or *hope* for better health, or *hope* to improve your financial situation. You give up all involvement and responsibility. You just give up.

There are times when hope has a place in your life and your spiritual and mental process. One never wants to lose hope for your child's continued happiness in life or hope for world peace.

There is a place for hope.

When it comes to your success and things over which you can or could have input and control, you need to **expect**.

My expectations are the basis of my success. Despite the hardships in my life, I can honestly tell you with unwavering confidence I have *never* just been satisfied with what I have so far.

*I wake up every day expecting success.*

I wish this were an audio book so you could hear the passion in my voice in the words that you are reading right now: I have never entertained a lifestyle of decrease; I have never thought to myself, "this is it." You absolutely, without question deserve your achievements and there is nothing wrong with waking up every day expecting exactly that!

Sashin Govender is a prime example of someone who internalized the concept of expectation at a young age. He accompanied his father to my seminars before he was a teenager, and he was not a shy, self-conscious 12-year old. Sashin sat up front and gave me every ounce of his attention. He put my teachings to work as soon as he was able and hit his first million by the time he was 20. Now, at 23, he is a multimillionaire and speaks on stages around the world.

As he was getting started, he called me almost every day. He never had a little voice in the back of his head that told him that he was bothering me, that it was too many phone calls, that he needed to dial it back. I recognized his hunger and mindset and I gave him direct access whenever he wanted.

Sashin was very young when he heard the concept *expectation to increase*. He was not jaded or tired; he hadn't grown up with limitations on his future. He knew that if he focused on limitation, that's what he would get.

He works like he is broke, every day, and he never stops to count his successes or rest on his laurels. Because he internalizes his expectation to increase, he's growing exponentially, and he'll have his first million-dollar year within two years.

There is so much power in *expectation*. Getting you to the mindset of expecting results will catapult you into a life that most people only dream of having. I want you to get to the mindset and determination of success in the exact same way that when you take a breath you *expect* oxygen, the exact same way that you *expect* a chair to hold you up when you sit down, the exact same way you *expect* the electricity to work when you turn on the lights.

You need to have that exact same expectation for personal triumph. Every day of your life you should wake up with an expectation of success.

It can start for you now. Inspect what you expect! Everyday, *expect* increase and I promise you, *your personal Break Through is imminent!*

# Biography

Johnny Wimbrey is a speaker, author, trainer, and motivator, working with sales teams, high-profile athletes, politicians, and personalities around the world.

He has launched three companies—Wimbrey Training Systems, Wimbrey Global, and Royal Success Club International—and heads a sales team of thousands in more than 50 countries, overseeing an active customer database of half a million families.

Johnny shares his powerful message through speaking engagements around the world. He also has a wide media following and has appeared as a guest expert and panelist on television shows including the *Steve Harvey Show, E! News,* and *The Today Show.*

Johnny's first book, *From the Hood to Doing Good,* has sold more than 200,000 copies in printed and digital editions.

Johnny has collaborated on several other books including *Conversations of Success* and *Multiple Streams of Determination;* combined, they have more than 500,000 copies in print.

Johnny regularly speaks for non-profit organizations and reunites children with their families from whom they've been separated for years due to government action. He and his wife, Crystal, are co-founders of Wimbrey WorldWide Ministries, a non-profit which has built six schools in Central America and helped fund water purification systems in Africa.

# Contact Information:

Johnny D. Wimbrey
Master Motivation/Success Trainer

MEMBER

NATIONAL
SPEAKERS
ASSOCIATION

<u>Most Requested Topics:</u>
Motivation/Keynote
Overcoming Adversity
Youth Enrichment
Leadership/Sales

## www.johnnywimbrey.com

 @Wimbrey

 @Wimbrey

 @Wimbrey

 JohnnyWimbrey

 @Wimbrey

 LinkedIn@Wimbrey

# CHAPTER TWO

# REDEFINING "NO"

## Transforming Failure and Rejection into Unimaginable Success and Boundless Opportunities

### Dana L. Mendenhall

A s far back as I can remember, I have been a natural-born leader. Emerging from a God-given source of determination and perseverance, it is my life's calling to use my position and my voice to lead and advocate on behalf of others. As you engage with me throughout this chapter, I hope you gain earth-shattering clarity and a renewed sense of purpose regarding your calling. I also hope you harness the power to seize every opportunity to *redefine "no,"* thereby creating unimaginable success and boundless opportunities in your life.

## The Beginning

The daughter of a chemist who instilled in me the value of problem solving and executing well-devised plans, I witnessed my father's daily example of sacrifice and hard work. He inspired me to pursue my life's dreams, no matter the obstacles encountered. My father referred to me as "the Pete Rose of baseball" as he watched me toil over tasks until I mastered them.

Dad also described Babe Ruth as "a gifted player to whom the game of baseball came naturally."

"Babe Ruth had baseball in his veins," Dad proclaimed, and he likened the road to greatness to the road to failure. Dad continued by emphasizing that discipline and perseverance—or the lack of them—determined the destination. Rose, unlike Ruth, achieved his greatness by dedicating his life to studying and practicing the game of baseball. Rose's discipline earned him the distinguished title of all-time Major League Baseball Leader in hits, games played, at-bats, outs, singles, and three World Series rings. My father taught me that Rose also served as a sober reminder of the importance of mastering your craft and not allowing your craft to master you. Despite his unmatched talent, Pete Rose was permanently ejected from baseball for gambling.

Today, my father still challenges me to work harder and longer than the competition, to persevere and never quit until the job is done, and to maintain a healthy curiosity about life and business. Dad and I believe dedicating our resources to causes greater than ourselves is the key ingredient for a successful life.

Also the daughter of a gerontologist, I watched my mother embody service as a cornerstone of her character. For nearly 40 years, she served seniors. She tirelessly dedicated her time and talents to those who often could not help themselves. Whether she ensured the electricity remained on in countless households or demanded warm meals and coats for everyone she encountered, the actions my mother took reinforced the importance of serving others.

As I inherited a perfect balance of the chemist and the

gerontologist, it will come as no surprise that even as a young child I practiced the same values that I demonstrate today as a global leader and agent for change.

One sunny fall day during reading class, our teacher's face turned red and flushed as she lost her breath and fell over in her chair. My classmates and I were frightened at what was happening to Mrs. Blaylock. I didn't comprehend what was happening, but I jumped up and ran down the hall to the principal's office to plead for help. The ambulance was called, and paramedics put Mrs. Blaylock on a gurney, removed her from our classroom, and rushed her to the hospital.

My classmates and I were left alone in our classroom by the distracted adults; we were paralyzed by fear and in a state of disbelief. At that moment, the leadership and advocacy lessons my father the chemist and my mother the gerontologist instilled in me began to work. I moved to Mrs. Blaylock's chair at the head of the table, quickly scanned her lesson plan, and began to execute it. Together, my classmates and I returned to a state of normalcy. We had completed our reading assignment by the time a teacher's aide finally arrived to oversee us.

When Mrs. Blaylock returned to school, she set in motion a force of positive reinforcement and praise that would follow me throughout my high school years.

# The Transition

Although transitions can be painful and lonely, I embrace each one as an act of self-love that produces growth, courage, and self-confidence. To successfully **get** through transition, I must **grow** through transition. Transition void of **pain** produces little to no **progress**. The other side of transition is where I achieve my greatest accomplishments.

As I transitioned from my teen to young adult years, life began to present challenges that required more than simple "yes" or "no" responses. Simply put, the challenges became increasingly difficult and each "no" began to outweigh each "yes." Before heading to college, I experienced success after success, and earned awards and rewards that assured me I was on the right track. Success became a habit I took for granted in exchange for hard work. After all, success was ingrained in my DNA.

That is, until transition set in. I began my first semester of college, and for the first time in my life, I struggled with academics.

I vividly remember confidently walking into a 300-seat lecture hall full of eager students just like me. I headed to the front of the room to ensure the professor could hear and see me if I had a question. I took copious notes class after class and was sure I had over-prepared for my first college exam. Then, the day of transition came upon me: A large "D" was scrawled across the top of my chemistry exam in bright red ink. I was completely mortified and barely could hold back my tears. I sat in class in a state of disbelief, disappointment, and embarrassment. Slowly, I gathered the determination to speak with the professor about my grade, contemplating and praying about each word I would say.

I went to his office, and prefaced my case by stating how proud I was to be a Fighting Texas Aggie after graduating at the top of my high school class and carrying a full load my first semester of college. After setting up my credentials, I shifted to the struggle I was experiencing despite hours of studying, and I explained my shock at getting a D on my first exam. I was serious as I told my chemistry professor the only D that ever appeared on my exams during my entire academic career to date had been the D in Dana where I wrote my name.

My professor may have chuckled and smirked a bit as he uttered five simple words and ushered me out of his office: "Welcome to the real world."

As the door closed behind me, my sadness and disbelief transformed into anger and determination—anger that he blew me off, and the determination to prove him wrong by earring an A in his chemistry course. After transitioning from my high school study methods to the more rigorous college techniques, I joined study groups and exam prep sessions, and met with colleagues who shared old exams.

My hard work, underscored by my unshakable faith, earned me a B in chemistry. Although I fell short of my goal of earning an A, I learned invaluable lessons that would catapult me to higher levels of achievement. I discovered I am cut from the cloth of perseverance. I possess the grit to tackle each challenge I encounter. I have the ability to transform the doubts and criticisms of others into the fuel needed to achieve my goals. I reject failure, flip it on its head, and pursue the necessary paths to achieve the seemingly impossible.

Embracing transition enabled me to graduate with more than a dozen job offers, one of the highest counts in my graduating class, and connected me with countless disruptive change agents who introduced me to unimaginable career opportunities.

The silver lining is this: What appeared to a "no" was instead an opportunity designed for me to transition to a higher level of thinking and devise alternative plans that resulted in a "yes!"

# The Mindset Shift

After five successful years of increasing responsibilities, multiple promotions, and diverse functional roles in a Fortune 50 company, I pursued the unthinkable—a transition from the technical to the commercial side of business. The career path I desired was with the customers I had the privilege to serve.

As a left-brain-dominant engineer, I drafted a career plan that moved my path to a right-brain-dominant sales role. Though it took thirteen interviews, I finally persuaded my company to place a bet on me as a medical device sales representative, working on commission rather than salary. That occurred at a time when the path from technical to commercial roles was paved with incomplete and unsuccessful assignments. Quite frankly, had I not developed the grit and perseverance to fight until I win, I, too, would have been a victim of a regrettable transition.

My new career as a sales representative began poorly. I took a technical mindset into a non-technical world and attempted to be successful. I failed at customer-centricity and focused solely on the features and benefits of our products. I spoke more than I listened. I gave up and moved on to the next opportunity at the first sign of rejection. After one month in my role, my paycheck offered a rude awakening to my poor performance. The numbers on the stub reminded me that if I did not sell, I would not eat.

I correlated my poor selling skills with failure and each customer rejection with personal defeat. My division manager, a brilliant leader and mentor, called me and emphatically stated, "Dana, you are working hard, but not smart." He stressed the importance of connecting and understanding customer needs versus regurgitating features and benefits of products and services.

Most importantly, he addressed my inner defeat by encouraging me to adopt his "24-hour rule." His rule described the mindset and approach winning sales representatives use when they're face-to-face with rejection. "After you receive a negative response from a customer, simply walk away and place the decision aside for 24 hours. Revisit the decision with a new mindset and pursue another approach," he insisted.

I skeptically applied the 24-hour rule after several unsuccessful sales calls. To my surprise, not only did I win the business, but also I won the trust and respect of my customers. My experience proved my manager's wisdom: *Rejection is typically resolved when refreshed minds devise alternative solutions to customer objections by simply "being the customer."* He knew there was a lesson and an opportunity behind every *No*.

After I overcame my initial fears of failure, hunger, and being broke, I accelerated my learning and improved my performance; by year's end, I'd climbed from the bottom of the sales roster to be "Rookie of the Year." I continued improving and became a reliably top-performing, award-winning sales representative.

I attribute my successes to my manager who taught me **"*No*" never means NO; it simply means "not now." Wait 24 hours and act—and not the same way. Try plan B, C, and D until you *succeed*.**

# Redefining "No"

I discovered my secret to success. My life is filled with countless opportunities to transition, shift my mindset, and transform failure and rejection into success and opportunity. I embrace *redefining "no"* not only as my personal mantra, but my lifestyle. As I climbed the corporate ladder from Industrial Engineer in Texas to Vice President of Marketing for Europe, the Middle

East and Africa for one of America's most admired companies, I tackled numerous challenges that reinforced my personal and professional growth through the power of *Redefining "No."* Learning to redefine "no" initially caused me to doubt my intelligence, question my self-confidence, and grow weary of hearing my voice. Constantly running into brick walls of rejection and brushing off failure only to repeat the same pattern can seem like an insurmountable task for even the bravest at heart. When learning to redefine "no," I unlearned life-long lessons regarding failure and rejection. I forged new paths, and upon arrival at the juncture of **defeat** and **breakthrough,** accelerated in the direction of **breakthrough.**

I boldly volunteered to be an agent of change who:

- Embraced a vision others could not see
- Seized opportunities others rejected
- Disrupted the status quo and created a new reality
- Utilized self-doubt and fear as fuel to make the impossible possible
- Drowned out voices of defeat and criticism to magnify the voice of opportunity
- Transformed failure and rejection into success and opportunity

My journey has afforded me the highest highs and the lowest lows, and each challenge faced has been worth every painstaking, character-building, life-changing moment. I would not change one thing.

If a girl from Little Rock, Arkansas, can learn to live the life she dreamt by **redefining "no"** to mean **"not now, not** *that* **way"** and create unimaginable success and boundless opportunities, so can *you*!

# Biography

Dana Mendenhall is a global health-care leader with more than 20 years of progressive experience, highlighted by an extraordinary record of achievement. She earned a BS in Industrial Engineering from Texas A&M University, and an MBA from Northwestern University's Kellogg School of Management.

By redefining "no," Dana offers readers a first-hand account on how a *do or die* mindset transforms rejection and failure into success and opportunity. She reminds readers of their right to a prosperous life and inspires them to pursue this life with every fiber of their being.

A native of Texas, Dana resides in Switzerland.

# Contact Information:

email: dana@redefiningno.com
email: bookings@redefiningno.com

# CHAPTER THREE

# Living Life
# on Life's Terms

## Henry Bronson

They say you don't get to choose your parents, but according to the records I was destined for the Winner's Circle. I had the classic upper-middle-class American Dream ahead of me. The circumstances were set up for a storybook ending. At least that's what I imagined.

It was pretty clear to me early on that my family was definitely well off. My dad's family was old. When we talk about coming over on the boat, it means the "Hercules" in 1628 with the London Company. No huddled masses here. The family was fruitful and multiplied. Bronson's settled New England, Michigan, and the Midwest.

My dad entered Union Theological Seminary in New York and eventually became an Episcopal minister. He met my Mom, who also was studying at Union. I am not sure what she was doing there, because it was forty years before women could be ordained as Episcopal ministers or have their own passport. I do know that she had a fine education and a lifelong love of learning. In any case, mom and dad were married at my grandmother's house in Bearsville, New York, in 1948.

Like most childhood memories, mine are a little fuzzy. But I do recall having a pretty normal time with two older brothers and a sister living in a nice house in Lexington, Kentucky. I think I was oblivious in the way a happy toddler can be. Some of my most vivid memories are very disparate. I remember hearing of the movie *Goldfinger*. It was a scandal because the actress who got painted gold was naked! And *Cassius Clay* was now *Muhammed Ali*. There was a lot of tension outside our Kentucky home because of the national civil rights movement, too. I recall talk of threats to my dad because he "said some things," which meant he may have spoken up about racial equality in a sermon. I am proud of him for that.

I don't remember exactly when it all went down, but the shit hit the fan in the form of a whirlwind of activity. We left Kentucky. My brothers and sister were away at school. My mother and I ended up in Cambridge, Massachusetts. Dad was gone. Apparently, he fell for another woman and set up housekeeping with her. Mom was in shock, and I hated kindergarten.

After a couple of years in Cambridge, Mom decided to move close to her mother in Woodstock, New York, in 1967. I got right into the third grade and did the things most kids do. I was pretty good and managed to develop almost normally. I did not see much of my brothers as they were away at a prestigious boarding school in New Hampshire. We would all meet up in the summer at the family cottage on Squirrel Island in Maine, an amazing place. Two miles from the mainland, one hundred or so families, ocean, woods, boats, and a lot of parties. *Summertime and the livin' is easy.* Meanwhile, my dear sister got the teenage rebellion bug and went to live with my Dad. I missed her.

In 1972, Mom decided to move again and I don't remember exactly why. This time, the destination was France. My mom had courage, I will give her that. See, I don't think I would have taken me anywhere. I was not really a complainer, but I sure was an asshole. I was twelve years old and thought I knew a lot.

Eventually, I had to go to the local French school, riding my bike there like a little French kid. They had discipline, awesome lunches, and spoke French, and I liked one out of three. I sucked in English class, ironically, because the teacher learned English in the United Kingdom and I spoke American English. It also didn't help that I was a punk. The head of school had a meeting about my attitude. I had to correct it, try not to torture the English teacher, and stop teaching the French kids American curse words.

To those kids, America was kind of mythically cool. I picked up on that and allowed myself to become a curiosity. My French got really good real fast. I found the cool kids to hang with. I listened to Led Zeppelin, smoked cigarettes, tried to get a moped to replace my bicycle, and settled for a leather jacket and a ten-speed.

Thrown into the mix were these great meals in ordinary places, which showed me that food was a big deal. I always enjoyed a good meal, but French food sparked something in me. Add my enjoyment of food to the fact that my mom wanted to see places and you get some great travel. My brothers came to visit. We took some great trips.

For the summer, we moved to St. Germain, just outside of Paris. I think the apartment owner in Menton doubled the rent in July and August. Vive la capitalism. We had an apartment in a funky old house and the landlord was a daughter of the famed French aviator Louis de Breguet. My best memory of that time was a trip to London. Having been allowed to go into Paris on my own, it was only natural that in London, I went on a solo journey to the Royal Air Force Museum in Hendon. I was a huge fan of the Battle of Britain, so that was really cool.

Here's the thing. I was 13. Who would let their teenager navigate solo in foreign countries on public transit? How many kids do you know who are equipped for such a thing today? I was using paper maps on the streets, interacting with strangers, and doing it all without a cell phone. Cool, right? I would do it again in a heartbeat.

Through these experiences, I became excited about food and cooking, travel, art, scenery, and culture. I love to learn and experience new and different things and to try new food and discover new people and places. Did I mention that my career path was to the kitchen?

We left France abruptly. One night, an owl was hooted right outside our apartment. You know what that means. Then, the phone rang at first light. My mom's father, Gus, had passed away. It was a blur. While Mom was not super close with him, and I'm not sure if he and my grandmother actually were married, I do know that Grandma was upset, so back to Woodstock we went.

In case you haven't heard, there was a party going on in Woodstock at that time. The Seventies were rocking. My mom started to find solace in the bottle and I got a little wild. Okay, a lot wild. I was in junior high and most of my friends were juniors and seniors in high school. I got into some shit. We were part of the subculture.

I got a job cleaning the kitchen at night at the legendary restaurant/music venue Joyous Lake. I saw so much crazy stuff and heard such incredible music it would blow your mind. I went to work at 11 p.m. and got home at 7 a.m. or 8 a.m. My friend Jon and I would hang with the artists and I would finish the kitchen clean up.

I also got a dishwashing job for a French chef at his restaurant Le Bistro—classic French food, about 30 seats. I knew all the food and spoke the lingo. The chef managed to make an old Garland range blow up on him, giving him second-degree burns on his arms and face. The restaurant called me and said I would be doing the cooking while the chef recovered. I soon was creating pot au feu, onion soup, beef wellington, coq au vin, crème caramel, and mousse au chocolat. I was *in*. Anthony Bourdain described it for us. We were *Pirates*. I have had a restaurant job ever since.

High school was a classic blur. I skated through academically, graduated early, and partied my brains out. Something happened to Mom, too. Her heart was broken and the effects were showing. The liquor store did well and our house did not. I stayed away as much as possible. If I was home and Mom was "in one of her moods," chances were high that it was going to be ugly. She was in such pain and had no one to talk to but bourbon. Then, the two of them would gang up on me. When you feel like shit, the way to feel better is: (1) Make sure everyone knows you feel like shit, (2) Share your misery, because misery loves company, and (3) Get stumbling drunk because alcohol is a solution which dissolves all your problems.

These were the coping skills I learned and applied.

I was accepted by some good colleges, and I chose University of New Hampshire. Away at school, I aligned myself with some of the best of the best party animals. I had plans to use languages (French and Spanish) and my business skills (I may or may not have at different points purchased and sold certain types of recreational substances for profit), study abroad, get an MBA and do whatever it was those people did. My downfall? With a classic alcoholic mentality, I managed to alienate my French literature professor, who was in charge of the junior year abroad program.

I did what any sane person would do. I took a sous chef job offer with a friend and spent the rest of any money I had for college on alcohol and drugs. Thank God I could work like a rented mule and could cook my ass off.

For ten years, I was a cooking and drinking machine. I spent a few years with my buddy, Bill, and then took a great job with my mentor, Tony, for another three years. I then had the opportunity to join a world-class team in New York City. I learned a ton, screwed up a good job, didn't get another great job, tried crack cocaine, did other crazy shit, and met my amazing wife, Dina. She's pastry, I was savory. We traded cookies for cigarettes and talked about our coworkers.

We got out of the city. We opened a restaurant. We survived and made a life. My drinking almost ruined everything. Then, after a crazy, crazy night with Courvoisier involved and hazy memories, I woke up on the floor with a sprained ankle, a blanket (thanks, Dina) and a head that hurt so much it felt like a Mack dump truck was running inside and the dump bed was opening and closing. Bang! Bang! Bang!

I opened one bloodshot eye and said, "Please help me." I was alone by the way. I am pretty sure I really meant it because a power greater than myself, who I choose to call God, has kept me away from a drink one day at a time ever since February 16, 1990.

It turns out I lived a few miles from the birthplace of the co-founder of Alcoholics Anonymous and there was a guy there who was bringing the dilapidated building back to life. He became my sponsor and mentor. He pretty much saved my life. I was on the skids spiritually. Mentally, I was a little shaky. Emotionally? Well let's just say that there were times when my humanity was questionable. I had hit bottom and managed some pretty good lateral movement for quite a while. Hitting bottom turned out to be one of the greatest blessings of my life because it became the solid foundation of my program of recovery.

Was that a breakthrough? Yes, indeed. I am grateful every day. Alcohol is only a symptom. The Big Book (AA) says we must get down to "causes and conditions" and I had a few. I was/am definitely my own worst enemy.

After nearly 30 years of sobriety and some introspection, I think that my desire to bend reality by drinking and using drugs "recreationally" really came from the trauma of my family being dismantled and my lack of coping skill development. I think I did okay as a seven-year-old boy. The problem is that I did not evolve beyond that. I really allowed resentment to run my life and I made decisions based on stuff I made up. That's one thing when you are a kid but it's a whole different thing when you are grown up and expected to do adult stuff.

To describe it simply, I made stuff up and believed it. Better still, I acted on that. We do it all the time. We design elaborate outcomes and scenarios based on fiction. When we see what's real, we deny, justify, or dismiss it as not applicable. The fantasy is so much better than the real thing, right? For people who are completely well adjusted, that may never happen. Good for them. Meanwhile, the rest of us are finding our way and the map is upside down, the page is missing, the GPS signal is lost, or someone changed the nice English lady's voice to Mandarin Chinese and she's telling us "Zuhuan zuo (left turn . . .)."

I believed my Dad was coming back and when he did not, I got pissed at him—really pissed. Not only was I abandoned by him, I was left with this crazy mother in a crazy town with a crazy life. On some level, I just wanted to be normal and I had no idea what that was. So, I embraced abnormal, in the sense that I rebelled and decided I would do whatever I wanted.

It was not a conscious decision. I did not wake up one day and decide to become a functional alcoholic. The cunning and baffling thing about alcohol is that when it gets you, it owns you. The disease of alcoholism is real. It's not simply about drinking. It's about having a hole in the soul and filling it with booze. It's about being controlled by a substance. Don't get me wrong. I had a blast, from what I remember.

Today is different. I know it is, even though I am on the inside looking out. I can't undo what I did, nor what was done to me. I can change how I interpret, understand, and most importantly, how I behave. I do not need to allow my past to define me. Do you hear the *Serenity Prayer* in there?

Today and every day I thank God and ask for knowledge of His will (stay with me, it's complicated and simple at the same time) and the power to carry it out. I was instructed by the guy who was my sponsor to pray every day. I didn't have anything to lose, so why not, right?

Today, I am a husband, a father, a chef, and business owner. My wife is a rock. I am eternally grateful. My kids are awesome. I can't express the love I have with words. I can still cook my ass off. Even though I am unemployable (a fact I confirmed with the last job I had a few years ago), I employ and support my staff and do my best in the community. Over the years, hundreds of people have been on my payroll and part of the family. Some are doing great, some I have not heard from, and some I don't want to hear from (and they might not want to hear from me), but all have had an impact on me. Thanks to all of them for helping me grow as a human.

Today, the breakthrough is about showing up and living life on life's terms. It's about having a past and getting past it. It's about raving a rational definition of normal.

Before AA, in many ways I decided I was a victim and I allowed that to influence how I behaved.

Today, I get to choose what defines me. And you should do likewise. Regardless of how hopeless it seems at times.

Today, I can choose gratitude.

Today, I get to understand, rather than be understood.

Today, the breakthrough is that, as Emmylou Harris said, *normal* is just a setting on a washing machine.

# Biography

Henry Bronson was born in Boothbay Harbor, Maine, grew up in Woodstock, New York, and New York City. A Chef, Traveler, Author, and Speaker he has been a student of life and continues to accumulate and dispense wisdom and fine food from Bistro Henry, the Vermont restaurant he owns with his wife Dina. When not in the kitchen or holding court, he can be found on the slopes, scuba diving, or seeking out the next great meal somewhere on the planet.

# Contact Information:

Henry Bronson
PO Box 1565
Manchester Center, VT 05255
henry@bistrohenry.com
802.688.6879
www.facebook.com/bistrohenry1
Instagram @henrytbronson

# CHAPTER FOUR

# Connect
# With Your Soul

**Avery Washington**

Throughout the years, I have learned to connect the desires of my soul with my personality by reflecting on many experiences in my life from the past and present. The process has allowed me to realize that my true purpose and passion are embedded within my soul, and if I want to achieve greatness, I must trust and follow the path of my soul's desires. It is my opinion that our lives will present us with events and relationships that are very meaningful and purposeful. Developing a high level of consciousness will lead us down the path to the desires of our soul, thus leading us to our breakthrough.

As I reflect on my life, I have come to realize my experience of being born and raised in New Orleans, Louisiana, in a single-parent home was a great blessing. I was an only child, and my mother, Diana Washington, worked long strenuous hours to provide for me and went to school to improve our future. As a toddler, much of my time was spent being raised by Big Momma, my great-grandmother Rachel Barnes, because my mother needed someone she could depend on to help take care of me. The unconditional love I received from Big Momma was a tremendous blessing to my mother and me for sure. Some of my happiest memories are of long conversations with Big Momma as we walked to the bus stop on our way to church on Sundays. We often spoke about the lessons from Sunday school and decided on the meal we would cook for dinner that day. I lobbied for mustard greens and cornbread because they were my favorite foods. Big Momma and I used our fingertips to mash our cornbread together with our greens and I sprinkled a little sugar on top of mine, because I liked my greens to be sweet.

Big Momma was extremely proud of me, and she always introduced me as her great-grandson to everyone we met. Her strong sense of pride was very inspiring, and it instilled a strong sense of pride, that's still deeply rooted within me. I truly enjoyed the quality time we shared; we established a bond that will forever be a part of me and will never go away. I'm very grateful to my mother for introducing me to the love of Big Momma, because her love and guidance were an exceptionally positive impact on my upbringing.

My mother's sisters stepped in to watch me from time to time, and so did my grandmother and grandfather as I got older. I have memories of collecting aluminum cans with my grandfather and making trips to the recycling plants to exchange the cans for cash. He enjoyed professional wrestling and we watched it together on television hours at a time. His favorite wrestler was Junkyard Dog, a 300-pounder who wore a dog collar and a silver chain. My grandfather was a great man and I'm certain much of my character and hard-work ethic stem from him.

When I was just eight, my father was murdered in the streets of New Orleans. Someone shot him multiple times and left him for dead. I never had a father-son relationship with him, so I didn't feel any pain from his death, and when my mother told me about his murder, it was as though she told me about the death of a stranger.

She asked, "Do you want to attend your father's funeral, Avery?"

I thought she probably wanted to go, so politely (but without much enthusiasm), I told her, "If you want to go, I will go."

We did attend, but when I didn't see any emotion from her, I didn't show any, either. I shed no tears when he was buried, and my life continued on without him.

Poetry books by Helen Steiner Rice, encyclopedias and works of art were always arranged throughout the home in which my mother and I lived by ourselves during my preteen and adolescent years. She always emphasized the importance of reading to me. I had no siblings, so when my mother went to work, I often read her books of poetry to keep me company.

The relationship that my mother and I share is incomparable. She taught me to have respect for women and to handle their hearts with care. My mother also raised me to be a man of integrity and to never allow anyone to disrespect me. Her strength, intelligence and independence has always had an empowering impact on my life.

I watched my mother go from working in hard hats and steel-toe boots to wearing a lab coat as she educated herself and became a chemical analyst. She always strove to achieve more so we could live a better life. There was nothing that could stop her from achieving her dreams. I learned so much from her over the years and I'm forever thankful.

After graduating from high school in 1990, I moved to

Houston, Texas, to attend Texas Southern University, and I stayed in Houston after graduation. When I was twenty-six, I fell in love with a gorgeous young woman named Kisha. Ironically, she too was a single mother, and her birthday was one day after my mother's. After we dated for about a year, I proposed to her in front of thousands of people when I was on stage with Bernie Mac. One year later we were married, and God blessed us with two more beautiful daughters within our marriage.

When I was in church one Sunday morning, Pastor Ralph Douglas West of The Church Without Walls began to speak about the gifts with which God has blessed us.

"We all are blessed with gifts from God and we must use these gifts as blessings to others, but some of us are holding on to these gifts," he said.

"When the government gives us student loans and we don't pay these loans back, the government takes the money back *anyway*. Maybe God needs to do likewise and start taking back the gifts that we continue to hold and not share with others."

At that very moment, I had the feeling he was speaking directly to me about my gift of writing. Over the years, I developed a serious love and passion for writing words of inspiration, but I never shared my work with anyone.

After listening to those powerful words from Pastor West, I heard two voices in my head directing me to do different things. The first voice said, "Avery, you need to go down to the local poetry lounge and share your writings with the audience."

The second voice disagreed. "Avery, it's football season and the Pittsburgh Steelers are playing. You should go home, relax on the couch, and watch the game."

I went to the poetry lounge.

That Sunday I began connecting with the desires of my soul. My decision to share my God-given gift led me to my first major breakthrough. This moment in my life reminded me of a famous quote from Dr. Martin Luther King, Jr., "Faith is taking the first step, even when you don't see the whole staircase." I had taken my first step toward greatness.

I wasted no time and began to research the business of book publishing. I found that many writers submit manuscripts to publishing companies, looking for approval of their work. My gift is from God, and I felt that His approval was good enough.

I always say, "Never seek the approval of man for the gifts that God has bestowed upon you with his very own hands." I love this quote! (Maybe because I wrote it.)

After completing thorough research on book publishing, I founded my own company, Happie Publishing. Do you wonder how I decided on the name Happie? Well, when I attended Texas Southern University, I had a great group of friends, and one of them, Lionel, had the sole responsibility of giving everyone else nicknames; his was Bean. One day he saw me and said, "You are always smiling, so I'm going to start calling you Happy!"

My cousin, Hilton, said, "That's your name now! When Bean gives you a nickname it sticks." The name was very fitting for me, so I didn't argue. I did change the spelling to *Happie* to give my new name a unique twist.

I continued to recite my writings at the local poetry lounge and I had established my publishing company, but had not yet published a single book. I decided to tell the promoter of the lounge, Varion Howard, also known as Se7en The Poet, that I was publishing a book of poetry. Before I knew it, he had introduced me to the crowd and announced that I had a new book coming out soon. After I gave my reading, Varion told me that I was invited to have my book signing at the lounge at no charge.

On my drive home, I wondered, "Why did he feel secure enough to tell everyone that I had a new book coming out when he hadn't seen a manuscript or any proof? He doesn't really even know me."

I also remembered hearing Les Brown say, "The universe works in your favor when you are doing what you were born to do!"

I wrote my first book, *Just Speaking My Mind, Spoken Word Poetry Vol.1,* and it did better than I had dared to hope. My book signing was a huge success and my very first book became a number-one bestseller.

I make a point of continuing to remain aware of the people I meet and conscious of the relationships that develop. As I reflect on everything that led up to publishing my first book with my own publishing company, I realize the more that I followed the path of my soul, the universe assisted me in building relationships and creating life events, both of which lead me to achieving the desires of my soul. This gives me confirmation and confidence that I am on the right path to more breakthroughs.

My undying love for my three beautiful daughters inspired me to write my second book, which also gave me a much deeper connection with my soul. The book was entitled, *Letters to My Daughters, Poetic Affirmations of Love from a Father.* This book was written from my heart and soul to my daughters, teaching them to embrace the love of God and self, so that they would never have the desperate need to seek love from man or anyone else.

When I shared the book with friends and family, it had an immediate emotional connection with everyone who read it. *Letters to My Daughters* also quickly became a number-one bestseller. When I was asked to be a guest on radio shows, I witnessed tears falling from the eyes of many different radio hosts. Some women said that the book touched their hearts because it reminded them of the relationships that they shared with their fathers. Fathers would share with me that they were using the book to help build closer relationships with their daughters.

As I continued following the path of my soul, I began to realize my life was going on a spiritual journey. I clearly remember one particular radio host, Ms. Evelyn Arrington; when we met at the radio station to discuss *Letters to My Daughters,* she opened her copy, and the book had sticky notes on almost every page. She biblically broke down my entire book to her listening audience and me. Her interview was an eye opener for me because it gave me more affirmation that I was connecting with the desires of my soul.

I'm most known for writing *Letters to My Daughters* and it has catapulted me into becoming a family advocate, and my expertise is specifically speaking on the significance of father and daughter relationships. In 2018, I was afforded the opportunity to speak before The Congressional Black Caucus in Washington D.C., and also was blessed to be a featured author at the NAACP annual convention in San Antonio, Texas.

Connecting with my soul and following its path has empowered me to start my very own publishing company, write five bestselling books, become a family advocate, and bless the lives of many with my God-given gift. Furthermore, I'm leaving behind a great legacy for my wife and three beautiful daughters.

*We all have been blessed with innate gifts from God to be used as blessings.* Connect with your soul and follow the path of your desires today; you will find your purpose and passion to do what you were placed on this earth to do.

I truly enjoyed sharing my story with you, and I look forward to soon reading about your own breakthrough!

# Biography

Avery Washington is an American poet, family advocate, speaker, publisher, and author of five bestselling books of inspiration. He is a passionate author who has combined his gift of storytelling and poetry into powerful collections of heartfelt writings to which we all can relate.

Washington is best known for writing *Letters to My Daughters: Poetic Affirmations of Love from a Father*, which profoundly speaks on the significance of father-daughter relationships. In 2018, he had the honor of talking about family advocacy before the Congressional Black Caucus in Washington, D.C., and at the NAACP Annual Convention in San Antonio, Texas.

Avery and his wife, Kisha, have three daughters, Diamond Janae', Breanna Mone', and Averianna Sydnie.

The family resides in Katy, Texas.

# Books by Avery Washington

*Letters to My Daughters:
Poetic Affirmations of Lovefrom a Father*

*Just Speaking My Mind: Spoken Word Poetry Vol.1*

*Mother: A Heartfelt Poetic Tribute Celebrating Single Mothers*

*Legacy: 2nd Edition of Profound Bestseller Letters to My Daughters*

*A Love Letter to Our Beautiful Black Women*

# Contact Information:

Website: www.averywashington.com
Email: inspiration@averywashington.com or
awashington1784@gmail.com
Instagram: @authoraverywashington
Facebook: www.facebook.com/AuthorAveryWashington
Twitter: www.twitter.com/authoraverywash
LinkedIn: www.linkedin.com/in/averywashington

# CHAPTER FIVE

# Choose Love, Choose You

## Christine Francis

I am different than most people. I am an empath, someone who has special understanding of the emotions other people are feeling. I am also a born lover and fighter with a fierce heart, so I not only love everyone, I *feel* everyone and everything deeply.

My history suggests I should be a statistic because I was born into a very complicated world with teenage parents. My mother was just 14 years old when I was born, and she did the very best she could to provide a good life for me. She sent me to private schools, private camps, and worked multiple jobs while putting herself through school. She did not want to become a statistic so she worked hard to become a good role model for me by getting her master's degree by the time I was 12 years old. We often struggled, but my mom always made sure we never went without.

My father was 16 years old when I was born. He was one of the most non-judgmental human beings I have ever known, except for when it came to himself. My dad was an addict, and was not always present in my life. In addition to that, he started another family after he and my mother split up which brought about multiple issues. My father lived life on his own terms for the most part. This included him feeding his demons consistently with alcohol and other substances. The rough lifestyle he chose led to him passing away at the young age of 52.

Both of my parents did the best they could with what they had and what they knew. They made sacrifices that most would not so that I could not just *have* a life, but *live* a life. For that, I am grateful.

While my basic needs were met, there was a lack of emotional support and stability. This happens to be extremely common with teen parents because their brains haven't fully developed nor have they learned proper coping mechanisms for life. As a result, I didn't learn to love or respect myself, which led to an assortment of abusive relationships and a heck of a lot of settling for less than I wanted or needed in my life.

For most of my life, I made decisions for myself based on how they would benefit other people. Some call that "people pleasing." One reason for that is I was born like this. I was born with the ability to light up a room without even trying. Another reason for my people pleasing was because the first time I told on someone for doing something that affected me negatively was extremely heartbreaking for me. I was four years old. My parents were separated at the time and my dad was living with his grandmother, the woman for whom I was named.

I had been playing in my dad's bedroom all night while he was out drinking. I remember it being really late when he got back so I jumped into bed pretending to be asleep. His girlfriend (whom he later married) was with him and they were both drunk as they climbed into bed with me. What happened next should never happen to anyone, let alone a little girl. They had sex while I was wide awake and in the bed with them. Because of the actions of my father and his girlfriend, I learned about both sex and addiction when I was just four years old.

In the morning, I called my mother and told her what happened. I swear to God she showed up at that house in what seemed like 2.5 seconds. I seriously thought she was going to kill my dad. I had seen her hurt and angry before this, but I had never seen her *this* way. Thinking it was my fault, I felt awful that I had gotten my daddy in trouble as I watched him sit there and sob while my mother destroyed his very being.

My four-year-old heart was filled with an overwhelming feeling of guilt and sadness for my dad. The only other time I remember seeing him sad was the day my mom kicked him out after she caught him cheating. The adult me understands that was the best move for us, but as a child, I never wanted to see my dad, or anyone, that hurt ever again.

That morning was when I began keeping secrets to protect others, even when it hurt me. Keeping secrets is not the right thing to do but it was all I knew how to do. I internalized a great deal of pain but instead of being angry and bitter, it made my passion (and life mission) to make the world the better place by helping people heal and live their best lives that much stronger. It is quite interesting how one incident set the tone for so many aspects of my life.

Being born a light into a world of dysfunction and chaos was more than challenging for me. Everywhere I turned, I was surrounded by addiction and abuse. So, I started using my gift of bringing love and light to others well before I even knew it was a gift. I would stand up for and advocate for anyone and everyone who showed disrespect to others. I did this all of the time, no matter who, what, when, or where. I did it even when it meant sacrificing my own needs. It wasn't easy for me. And often, it took a toll on my mental and physical health but again, this was all I knew.

Over the years, I grew really tired. I spent many years in psychotherapy, and while it kept me alive, it didn't force me to do the actual hard work on myself. Desperation did. Pain did. The fact that I felt comfortable in my pain just never sat well with me. I have experienced some of the darkest pains. I have endured trauma, alone. More times than I could count. And while it made me emotionally hard, in the sense that I didn't let people all the way in, I never stopped showing people love. I did not always care for myself in the same way.

I was molested and raped. I have been assaulted physically, sexually, and verbally more times than I can count by both men and women, both friends and strangers, throughout my entire life. I have been robbed. I have suffered emotional and physical abuse at the hands of people I loved. I have had a near-death experience due to a pulmonary embolism. I have attempted suicide a couple of times and experienced suicidal ideation about 100 times. I have been abandoned and betrayed. I have been financially abused. I have lost those I love through death and by growing out of relationships. I have been both without a vehicle and homeless due to self-sabotage.

In 2014, I went through a divorce. Shortly after my divorce, I ended an affair in which I was involved with a married man who I truly loved. That same month, my mother was institutionalized just days before her father—who had been like a father to me—died. Later that year, my own dad died unexpectedly, my mother went to prison four days after that, and then I lost my full-time job because I didn't have enough paid time off to handle both of their affairs.

It was one of the darkest periods of my life.

I passed through life not caring if I lived or died. But each day I somehow got up and fought for others, and in a sense, I guess, myself. Just two weeks after my father's death, I returned to my part-time job of counseling court-mandated domestic violence batterers. Because I had lost my full-time job, I increased my case load from approximately 30 men to about one-hundred court-mandated domestic violence batterers—yes, *batterers*, not victims. Even though I was broken, I gave all the compassion, love, and knowledge I had to these convicted batterers because loving others is what I do. The reality of it is, many of the men I counseled were victims of abuse which is why they were repeating the cycle. One of my favorite quotes (from an unknown author) is, "I did not come here to teach you. I came here to love you. Love will teach you." I truly believe that.

Love teaches and love heals.

I can't count all of the backward ways I got back up and on my feet. I know I'm 100% accountable for all of the ways I have screwed up and continue to screw up (or learn life's lessons) and try to avoid facing my pain. I have hidden in my work. I have allowed myself to be distracted by men. There were times I masked my pain with marijuana and alcohol. All of these bandages just prolonged the grieving and the healing. I was trying to take shortcuts to get where I needed to be, when in reality I was actually taking really long detours.

During the darkest days of my life, you would find me with pain in my heart and soul, but a big smile on my face, building up my clients, my family, my friends, and even strangers. I would remind them we are all dealt a hand and while some of us get some real shitty cards, we always have a choice. We can fold or we can play. I would hear my voice speak to them with such passion, conviction, and love.

Then I would ask myself, *"Why them and not you? Why are they worthy and deserving, Christine, and you are not?"* As silly as it sounds, I just didn't believe I deserved compassion or love. I was the *ONE* exception to my own rule.

As I have grown wiser, I have learned that I have full control of where I go and where I do not go in life. We all do. We have the choice to be a victim of our circumstances or to be the victor. We have a choice of whether or not we educate ourselves to do better and be better. Yet, we live in a society of broken, angry people who sit around watching television and expecting miracles to happen. I get it, I have been similar to that person.

What's even crazier is that we surround ourselves with these hurt people, wondering why we aren't going anywhere in life. If the people in your circle don't inspire you, you don't have a circle at all: What you have is a *cage*.

One of the best things we can do for ourselves is face the discomfort and pain of change. We need to get out of our comfort zones. We all have a choice and most importantly, we only live this life *once*. It is absolutely selfish for us to sit back and play it small. We *all* have a part to play. Every single one of us. No one is destined for a life of misery unless they choose that.

Change isn't easy, but a mediocre life isn't easy either. The thought of waking up at the end of my life and being filled with regret is scarier to me than anything else.

After all I have been through, I still choose love. I might not have cared whether I lived or died a time or two (or ten), but I was still listening to my heart and working to change the world one person at a time by loving hard. I love so hard and I always will. Do you know why? Because that is what I *choose*.

I CHOOSE LOVE.

Just like I choose to get back up. No matter how deep the pain, the heartache, the situation, I choose love and I choose life. You can, too. We can live our lives in mediocrity or we can make it the best life. The choice is always ours.

You must *move* differently if you want life to be different. It's okay if you don't know how! Like many of us, you weren't taught to live your best life. But what's great about that *now* is that you are aware. You understand you are in full control. You know that whatever you want can be had if you do whatever it takes.

YOU CAN LEARN TO BREAK THE CYCLE! You can learn from yourself! You can learn from those who have lived before you. You can learn from your family and friends. Really, you can learn from anyone who has what you want, whether it be wealth or true happiness. You can always learn more than what you know right now. And you should.

Of course, there will be storms, and the tide will most certainly change. Life isn't meant to be all smooth sailing and sunshine. Life can be really hard. How we react to it is what makes us or breaks us sometimes. No matter what, we get to choose. Since indecision is a choice in itself, you are making a choice whenever you choose to do nothing. I pray you choose yourself. I hope you choose to *live* and not just exist.

Just as I did, you will face adversity. I want you to choose love—and choose YOU—during those difficult times.

# Biography

Christine Francis graduated from the University of Rhode Island with a Bachelor's Degree in Psychology. Francis focused her attention on using her innate healing abilities, as well as her voice to counsel and be an advocate for those who suffered from a history of addiction and domestic violence. She dedicated several years to serving individuals with emotional and physical disabilities by guiding them to successful and meaningful employment.

Through her own personal experiences, Francis has learned how to love and respect herself. She has made it her life's mission to ensure others find their own healing path toward love and a healthy lifestyle. She is so passionate about making the world a better place that she has partnered with a company that has something everyone needs.

Her best is yet to come.

When not helping others, Christine enjoys the ocean, whether sunbathing near it, swimming or boating in it. She also loves traveling, food, spending time with loved ones (including her "furbaby" Mia), singing, and dancing.

# Contact Information:

Email: iamchristinefrancis@gmail.com
Website: worldwidebiohacker.com
Facebook: Christine D. Francis
Twitter: @christine0419
Instagram: @iamchristinefrancis

CHAPTER SIX

# Multiplying Our Impact

### Rose Nyarangi Shelley

The trajectory of our lives appears obvious looking back, but it gives us very little guide to our future. When I look back at my own path, it looks as though it led neatly to where I am now. But it was littered with choices: forks in the road, landmarks and land mines, uphills and downhills.

I grew up in the '60s and '70s in newly independent Kenya, the third of eight children and daughter of a hard-working civil servant who bundled us from one dusty town to another. Trailing along with my dad's postings, we seemed to be constantly on the move to new homes and new schools. Faced with new teachers and new friends, my sisters and I were always the newcomers. Mostly, we were welcomed but sometimes, we were forced to find our own ways to cope far from home, and I quickly learned to exploit my ability to connect with people.

My mother grew tired of the constant relocation and took herself back to the family farm where we stayed during school holidays. We fetched water from the well, shooed herds of elephants, and picked our own corn. The endless safaris in trucks and four-wheel-drives over the plains and mountains were an adventure, but this was our normal day-to-day life. Only in retrospect do I realize how privileged we were and that this wasn't how other children lived.

I must have been a rebellious child. I remember my headmistress telling me I would amount to nothing. Years later, I met her again at a class reunion.

"Do you remember me?" I asked.

"Remember you?" she responded. "How could I forget you!"

She remembered me as a troublemaker and a rulebreaker, and she labeled me a non-conformist. Instead, I saw myself as a risk-taker, an adventurer who experimented with novel experiences. I traveled to America not knowing anyone, armed only with the address of someone I'd never met. I quit my first job because I took offense at my boss, another because I was bored. While many people agonize over such decisions, they come all too easily to me. Fortunately, I had a good support network to stop me from straying too far out of line.

It was my contrary nature that took me out of a safe posting as a bank clerk and into the more exotic world of tourism and hospitality. I found people—and travel—a lot more interesting than money.

Driving to work one day, I stopped to talk to a young boy, Saidi, who sold nuts on the side of the street near the ferry. I asked him why he wasn't in school.

"So, I can take some money to my mother to feed my little brothers," Saidi told me.

Touched, I began to purchase his nuts and then returned them for him to resell. After some weeks, I asked to meet his mother. She sat in a mud hut nursing a baby while another played at her feet.

"Why isn't Saidi in school?" I asked her.

"I can't afford the fees," she told me.

When I offered to take care of school costs, she asked, "But if he goes to school, how will I feed my other children?"

That stopped me in my tracks. What a choice to have to make!

I'm sure my encounter with Saidi influenced many of the choices I've made since.

It was a difficult choice to move in with my sister Jayne to help care for her daughter, who was born with cerebral palsy. And not long after, I faced another fork in the road when I met the Englishman who would become my husband. For that, the choice was to keep my secure life on the Kenyan coast or venture into the unknown.

I took the gamble. I couldn't have guessed that years later, Steve and I would be still married, with a 24-year-old son, and living in the United Kingdom, or that my professional career would take some equally significant turns. You see, if you're averse to a bit of risk, if you prefer the proverbial comfort zone, you won't see opportunities when they pop up over your horizon. Opportunities don't come looking for you, you have to put yourself in their path.

Steve ran his own training business in Nairobi. He'd asked me repeatedly to get involved, but I always refused: "Over my dead body!" The idea of standing up and talking to a group of people filled me with dread. But one morning he called in a panic. One of the trainers had lost her voice and no one else was available. What could we do? Take a deep breath, pluck up courage, make a decision, and run with the new opportunity.

"OK, bring me the manual, I'll give it a go!" I said.

With my palms sweating, voice shaking, and heart racing, I soldiered on for two days. The rest is history, as they say. I'd found my calling. I loved it, and fortunately my audience loved it, too. That was twenty years ago. Since then, I've stood in front of audiences on hundreds of occasions to run training courses and deliver motivational talks. I've worked with leadership teams, sales personnel, business owners, university students, and school children. My work has taken me to many different countries. I've discovered I can create trust, deliver know-how and new ideas, and inspire people to action. People are hungry for opportunity and it has become my passion to help them find their own calling.

Living amid two cultures has proven to be a wonderful learning opportunity. My birthplace was a country struggling to find its place in the world. Now, I'm living in the United Kingdom, I see a country also struggling with its identity and a people who seem to have lost direction. Like many countries, the United Kingdom seems to be poorly led, with leaders who place their own interests above those of the people. Back home we suffer the depravations of a kleptocratic elite who drain the lifeblood out of the economy. Yet, we trust these same corrupt politicians with our health and our education, and, unfortunately, children frequently adopt them as their role models.

Education is the means by which people expect to improve themselves, but the school system is stressed to the breaking point. Kenya is a country where an average child has never owned a book. Reading is something you do only to pass exams. In rural areas, there may be no running water, no electricity, no supermarkets, and no public transportation. Children often walk miles to and from school and they do their homework by the light of a kerosene lamp. Kenyan kids have hopes, dreams, and ambitions like everyone else, but where can they find leadership and life skills to propel them into the world?

An opportunity arose to bring my training skills to bear on this dysfunctional world of state education. The concept was to develop a mentorship program and provide life skills training to teachers and school children to help inculcate ethics and values into our next generation of leaders. The program is called *Pata Kitabu* (Swahili for "Give a Book") and we use the award of books to incentivize and reward good behavior. Teachers and the children themselves become role models in ethical behavior. Over thirteen years, we've brought fifteen schools in Kenya's Rift Valley into the program, with more than eight thousand students, two hundred teachers, and close to five thousand parents and community leaders. Through this forum, I've had the great satisfaction of reaching out and making a difference. More and more people are asking how they can use the concept within their own communities.

It's a common perception that the so-called developed and developing worlds have different needs and standards of living, but that's not what I'm seeing. Both in the United Kingdom and in Africa, parents worry about raising well-adjusted children who can survive and prosper, with life skills that help them navigate the challenging world into which they are stepping. Instead it seems as though too many young adults are failing to benefit from their time at school and university. They are being thrown into a turbulent world without a moral compass, and they lurch by default into a life of dependency. It saddens me that the promise of a better life fizzles out in the absence of opportunity.

That is the kind of gap I like to try to fill through mentorship and coaching. I wonder how I can use my experience in Africa to help elsewhere, and what I might learn from here that I could take back to Africa, but it's hard to make a big difference alone.

If we can collaborate to reach and touch more young people, if we can enlist the help of more parents, and connect with more "shakers and movers," we will have a much stronger chance to make a difference in young people's lives.

It seems like a mammoth job but that's familiar territory. In my son's final term at his Kenyan school, parents were invited to join the class trip to climb Mount Kenya, the highest mountain in Kenya, second only to Kilimanjaro in the whole of Africa. In my usual way when faced with such a choice, I signed up right away. There I was, having the worst day of my life, and in retrospect one of the best. I couldn't breathe, I couldn't walk, I was freezing, and my head ached. I just wanted to get off that mountain. And although I could barely speak, I told everyone how I felt. One of the other parents—thanks, Ken!—took me by the elbow.

"When I take a step, you take a step," he said. "When I take a breath, you take a breath. And then we do it again. Slowly, one foot in front of the other."

And suddenly, there we were at the summit. I was the last in our group. Not everyone made it. And there was my son Neil, shivering beside a rock.

"Well done Mama, you made it," he said.

One of the toughest decisions I ever made was to leave my son in boarding school while my husband and I moved to another country to set up a new business. The writing was on the wall: The Kenyan economy was spiraling downward and taking our business with it. We spotted an opportunity in neighboring Tanzania and for several years, we commuted back and forth over a thousand miles each way to see Neil during the various parents' weekends and holidays. While Neil was at the school, I had the idea to run a "home away from home," acting as a surrogate parent for children whose real parents couldn't be with them. That meant that Neil had a lot of friends with him much of the time. He agrees that he ended up with a fabulous upbringing. We turned adversity into advantage.

It's often said that fear acts as an obstacle to achieving your goals. But for me, fear has been a motivator. I was afraid of that mountain. I was afraid we wouldn't be able to give our son the best education. I am still afraid of growing old or infirm without enough money to live on. Conquering fear demands a courageous decision making a positive action. If you don't act, if you don't take the plunge into the unknown, you guarantee you'll miss your goals. Yes, there are risks in following your dream, but I believe the biggest risk is not taking any risk at all.

As I've moved into a new chapter in my own life, new opportunities have presented themselves. I've been voted into a leadership role as a volunteer director in running our community-owned pub. It's the nerve center of the village. I've also been invited into a couple of youth mentorship projects, working with teenagers who need to learn about the wider world and the roles they might take in it. My own contrarian past is in no way defining my present, but it's a useful reference point.

Life is a journey. But without goals—destinations and stopping points on the way—it becomes directionless. Goals provide purpose, yet our dreams make the journey an adventure. It's my goal to help the children I work with, but it's my dream to travel more and make connections with people all over the world. It seems clear to me now that the riches we collect on our journey are not measured in money but in experiences and in the difference we make. Money may be important, but it's what we do with it that counts. My mentorship program needs financial support, and it's one of my goals to achieve financial freedom for myself. I'm already working on that. It will enable my projects to gain a life of their own and enable me to make a lasting impact on the people that come my way.

My choices now are simple; indeed they've already been made: travel the world and help people find opportunity, unblock their lives, and pursue their dreams. If this sounds like you, too, let's join hands and multiply our impact.

# Biography

Rose Nyarangi Shelley grew up in Kenya and graduated with a business degree before embarking on a sales career in the hospitality industry. She established an events management company and later joined her husband's training business where she found her calling as a motivational speaker, trainer, and coach.

She has worked with clients across multiple sectors and addressed audiences large and small, including management teams, sales personnel, non-profits, government institutions, United Nations agencies, colleges, schools, and women's groups. She has presented seminars in countries around the world including Kenya, Tanzania, Uganda, Rwanda, Ethiopia, Zimbabwe, Mauritius, and the United Kingdom.

Rose is a Managing Trustee of the Pata Kitabu Foundation, a non-profit mentorship program that provides training to teachers and life skills mentoring to school children in Kenya, incentivizing and rewarding good behavior through the award of books.

She serves as the overseas fundraiser for *Hidden Talents*, a children's rehabilitation center in Nairobi.

Now living in the United Kingdom, Rose leads a team of accredited representatives in a global travel and lifestyle club. She and her husband, Steve, are directors of Strategic Alignment Ltd., which provides consulting, coaching, and publishing services, and she serves on the board of her local community-owned pub, *The Anglers Rest*.

61

Rose's passion is to help people find opportunity, unblock their lives, and pursue their dreams. Her goal is to partner with people who share her vision of giving back in a practical way to an unequal and often unfair world.

# Contact Information:

Email: breakthrough@rosenyarangi.me
*Website:* rosenyarangi.me
Twitter: @rosenyarangi

CHAPTER SEVEN

# The Awareness of Greatness

### Jarray Davis

**M**any movies have been made about brave men embarking on a quest to find a treasure that either is lost or thought to be a myth. Of course, you realize all these movies are just metaphors for life. We're not truly searching for the Holy Grail or some crystal skull; instead, we're looking for the treasure buried within each of us. And just like the mythical treasures, the ones that exist within us are not easy to reach but are well worth the journey.

For me, it took a seven-year prison sentence to obtain the treasure of true awareness: the awareness of greatness. For you, the path could be much easier.

I didn't come from a broken home, or a poor, violent, drug-riddled neighborhood. I grew up with both of my parents—two people who attracted a lot of envy and hate because they'd done better than some of the people from their past. And what did I do? I basically wrapped and hand-delivered the opportunity for those people to point the finger at my parents, laugh, and say, "We knew you would fail at something."

I landed myself in a spot of trouble, resulting in spending

seven years of time around real criminals who were serving the better part of twenty-five years. I felt like a claustrophobic who is locked in a closet. Even though I was in the midst of hundreds of people, I felt alone and abandoned. In the free world when you're in an uncomfortable situation you have the option to walk away. I was *not* in the free world. Thankfully, the same dirt that's thrown on a casket to symbolize the end of life also gives birth to grass and flowers.

Nothing comes easy, right? After you make that long journey within and reach the treasure of greatness, you discover it's locked up behind a door. The door is not easily opened with a key; instead it's opened by carefully manipulating a three-number combination lock.

The first number is revealed when you get your mind right. That is accomplished through education, which does not necessarily mean obtaining a college degree. You can educate yourself in the comfort of your own home—just pick up a book or two.

The second number is revealed when you get your spirit right. To accomplish this, let go of jealousy, hate, and any other forms of negativity that weigh down your spirit. Become more in tune with the infinite, whether you refer to that as God or the universe.

The third number is revealed when you stop asking what the world can do for *you* and start asking what you can do for the *world*.

The first two numbers were revealed to me while behind the confines of prison steel and concrete. I once lived in a ten-man cell—I know, absolutely no privacy. Two nice guys took a liking to me. Every night they would flank me and attempt to instill positivity into my negative brain—but I wasn't interested. My heart wasn't in the right place. You have to be ready in order to receive, isn't that right? If I throw a ball in your direction, your hands should be out ready to receive. Otherwise the ball may fall short, or worse, hit you in the face. Every night these guys would lob an underhand softball my way, but it would fall directly in front of my feet.

These two guys invited me to a meeting of a group called the Five Percenters. I agreed to go, and hatched a plot to soak up all their secret knowledge and weaponize it against them. However, the joke was on me because my attendance at this meeting changed my life forever.

I can wholeheartedly admit that I have a problem. When I involve myself in something new, I tend to go all out. I go to the extreme with my dedication. When I say, "Get your mind right"—for you that may be reading a book every month or so— which is totally fine. In my case, I literally woke up learning. The foot of my bed was piled with books and pamphlets, and when I awoke, I would sit up, grab something, and start reading before I did anything else. I did the same thing at night—I couldn't lie down and go to sleep without learning something.

Don't get the impression that I was always in the mood. At times, I would have to force myself because I realized the more I learned, the more I realized I knew nothing. I knew less than Jon Snow from *Game of Thrones*. My brain broke down the knowledge like the body breaks down food, except that instead of growing physically, I gained a newfound understanding and awareness with every morsel of information I consumed.

I was keenly aware of the circumstance I'd created for myself, and I wanted nothing more than to change the outcome. A negative circumstance is like a paved road that comes to an end. Most people will turn their car around when they reach the end of the pavement, because they know it'll be a bumpy ride to their destination from that point on. But I'm telling you to pull your seatbelt tighter and hit the gas. Take those bumps and dips like a champ as you see the less-determined travelers getting smaller in your rearview.

After a failed strike by the prisoners, the powers that be shipped us off to other penitentiaries. As an inmate caught in the crossfire, I ended up in a prison located in Powhatan, Virginia. Because of the move, I was now separated from the Five Percenters who had changed my world. There were a few people on the new compound who claimed to be members but were clearly faking it—but that turned out to be a good thing. Being away from a bombardment of the same messages heard day-in and day-out allowed me to clear my mind. Having to rely upon myself allowed me to be more *me* than I'd been in quite some time. I was still digesting large quantities of knowledge, but my diet had changed. I sought a closer relationship with the Infinite—and I found it. That's when the journey took a different form. I wasn't driving on that bumpy road any more. No, I was flying over it. I had obtained the second set of numbers. All of this occurred at the most ideal time, because I was getting out.

For whatever silly reason, I thought getting out of prison would solve all of my problems. I'd spent so much time—a ridiculous amount of time—preparing for that moment, it was impossible for me to see freedom was just an illusion. Though I'd walked out of the prison gates, I was still very much incarcerated—and so was everyone else around me. We can be incarcerated by our thoughts, by our jobs, by our relationships, by our desires, by money, and never get free because we already *believe* we're free.

After I got out of prison, one of my older brothers helped me get a job cleaning and taking out trash at a hotel. I loathed the job because I'm more of a boss kind of person and the job required me to take orders from everyone. I'd just spent the last seven years constantly taking orders, and here I was trapped in that same position. To make it worse, my high school reunion was happening and as my classmates came to town, they stayed at the hotel where I worked. And guess who had to pick them up from the airport and carry their luggage? Me. So, I spent all my available time searching for a new job, but I was rejected every time I applied because of my criminal record.

Rejection is a monster scarier than the boogeyman. Rejection is designed to make you believe you are worthless, or at the very least, that your knowledge, skills, and talents are worthless. Rejection is a cold-blooded killer, one that will murder your hopes and dreams if you don't fight back. Society was causing me to become more familiar with rejection than I had thought was possible. Society wanted me to stop committing crimes, but society also did not want me to have a job that supported me.

My job paid $7.25 an hour, yet I had a seven-year-old who was my responsibility to support, along with $4,000 in back child support that accrued while I was in prison. I also had another $4,000 in court fines and restitution that had to be paid. The pressure was mounting.

The pivotal moment was not far away. I'd applied for a job at a company that was entertaining the idea of hiring me. After a couple of interviews, they'd called me in to fill out the necessary paperwork. There was a question on the paperwork about my background, and I'd answered it honestly. On my way out, I stopped by their front desk to make sure nothing else needed to be done. A young lady looked me in the eye without any emotion and said, "On your paperwork it says that you have a felony. Is that correct?"

I didn't know what the next step would be, so again, I answered honestly, "That's right."

"I'm sorry," she said without hesitation. "We don't hire felons."

I couldn't believe she was so blatant in her response. Usually companies lie and say that a felony doesn't necessarily prevent you from being hired, but then they never call you. What happened here was a slap in the face. I walked out of the building *fuming*. I think I must've sat in their parking lot for about thirty minutes with a full head of steam. I wanted nothing more than to go back in that building and let out some of my frustration—frustration that more than likely would have sent me flying backward in life.

But I didn't give in to my emotions. Shifts at the plant changed, and I still sat in the parking lot, thinking. Finally, an actual picture of a fork in the road became clear in my mind. Somehow I knew it was a fork on my journey to unlock my true potential. In one direction, there was the money I needed to survive and all of the risk that came with it. In the other direction, was continued rejection, humiliation, but also the soundness and stability of the straight and narrow path. I started my car and drove off, having calmed myself by making a decision.

To be totally honest, the straight-and-narrow option was not my first choice, but that was a brief mental detour. I knew I was responsible for putting myself in my current situation, and as my self-anger subsided and the elevator in my mind moved up to the top floor where it belonged, I knew I had to take the harder path. Though I despised my job, I went in every day, giving more and more of myself without complaints; without my hand extended. Sure, there was still rejection in the face of all that. There were other employees who abused their authority over me for their own entertainment. There were managers who went straight to the general manager to complain about me in an effort to sway his perception because they saw my tenacity, which made them feel threatened. But it didn't stop me.

That's when I received the third number for the lock. I became even more confident; even more determined. A promotion followed that took me away from the trash, cleaned me up, and placed me at the front desk in a suit. More rejection followed, as people felt I didn't deserve to be there.

On my part, more confidence and determination followed, which led to another promotion. I was given oversight as the general manager of not one, but *two* hotels. Something that had taken some people a decade to achieve was granted to me in less than half the time. It wasn't magic—it was following the three steps to unlocking my true potential.

Though this chapter is over, my story is far from complete. At the point of reading this, your story can make a plot twist—it's up to you! You are the author, and your decision-making is the pen that writes the story. Every great story starts with an outline, a clear direction on where the story will begin and end, point for point, and scene for scene.

Your story has already begun. Where do you want it to end? Create your plot twist today by unlocking your potential.

# Biography

Jarray Davis is the founder and CEO of Jarray Enterprises. A Virginia native and Maryland resident, he is the author of *After Attraction: Relationships Are Simple, Right?* as well as his memoir *Elevators in My Mind*.

Davis has been a hospitality management professional for more than ten years. Through the hospitality industry, Jarray learned the fulfillment of being in service to others: "There comes a point in life when you've received so much that your sights should be re-directed toward giving."

Jarray is also a motivational speaker catering to the educational and corporate markets.

# Contact Information:

Email: info@jarraydavis.com
Website: www.jarraydavis.com
Instagram: @jarray_davis

CHAPTER EIGHT

# A Continuous Journey

## Christina Velidou

My parents were farmers in a small village in northwest Greece, and they raised me with the love every person on earth should have. Our house held an extended family of thirteen: my parents and my twin brothers, our grandparents, my father's youngest sister, and an uncle with his wife and children.

What an experience! I learned to live in a community within my own house. We were taught to respect each other, respect the rules, and make sure we weren't in the way of the grown-ups when they discussed serious matters and made decisions for us all. Even then, I was always there to listen, as I found it fascinating to hear different opinions and think about the best outcome for all.

My twin brothers, John and Sakis, are five years older than me, and Sakis was born deaf. When he was young, my parents made the hard decision to send him away to a special school to learn to speak and communicate. On school holidays he came home, and those days when my family was united, were my favorite. The summer I was 9, Sakis came home to stay for good.

We were at the basketball court playing with other kids from the neighborhood when something happened that changed my life.

A neighborhood boy said cruel things about my brother and everybody laughed. It took me a heartbeat to react before I jumped on the bully, although he was bigger and older, I started punching him.

Sakis pulled me off the boy and asked, "What happened? Why are you behaving like this?"

I didn't want Sakis to be hurt, so I lied, "That boy said something bad about me." When Sakis turned on the boy I realized he could really hurt him, so I quickly said, "Stop! He's learned his lesson."

*I* was really the one who learned a lesson. I realized that my initial reaction was wrong, and violence could cause chaos. It made me think that there are other ways to deal with such people. At that moment, I knew *my brother is going to need me in his life.* Although I was younger, my duty was to keep an eye on him and make sure he wouldn't be bullied, at least not when I was around.

When I was 12, the people who ran our town's basketball program asked my parents if I could join the team. When they said, "No, Christina is too young," oh, how much I cried! Crying didn't do a thing to change their minds.

When I was 14, my town's football (soccer in the United States) team asked my parents for permission for me to join them. Their answer was *"No!"* again, but this time I wouldn't give in. I fought for my dream of becoming a professional athlete. I promised I would still be first in my classes if I was allowed to join, as this was their fear.

Plus, my parents wondered, "How can a girl play football?"

I can't blame them. It was a brand new concept, and not just in our little town. I told my parents, "What hasn't happened yet doesn't mean it will never happen." That convinced them, and I also kept my promise. When I asked my parents years later what had changed their minds, my dad said, "Your determination! The look in your eyes."

Mom added, "Your promise to still be first at school!"

Lesson taken! I was determined and ready to make the sacrifices and I felt I could accomplish anything. My journey in football was awesome! My bond with my teammates, my selection to the national team, pushing myself to become better and better, and my parents watching the games and being proud of me were vitally important.

My first coach, Dimitris, trained us to become better humans, not just athletes, and I will always be thankful. He taught us to use our brains, to think and evaluate all kind of information, to be humble, to work hard toward our goals and dreams, and to never give up. Last, but not least, was to support each other and be a family off the field as well as on it.

Our team from a tiny town in northwest Greece won the Greek championship and was one of the most competitive teams in the league for years. Our love for the game, even when times were hard, was as important as our hard work and commitment.

When I was nineteen, I moved to Crete for college to study tourism and hotel management; that's when I realized I love traveling as much as I love sports. I wondered, "How can I travel the world and make money at the same time?" The answer came fifteen years later.

During these years, my family had changes and challenges.

My brother John crashed his car, and we didn't know if he would wake up. We prayed to God, sleeping in our car just to be next to him at the hospital, counting days and believing each one would not be his last.

When he woke up, he had a brain injury, but he was

walking, talking, and smiling. He would not be the same, but he was still alive!

A teacher asked us a question on graduation day: *In which hotel department do you want to build your career?*

My fellow students wanted to be managers in food and beverage, reception, etc., but when it was my turn to speak, I said, *"None!"*

My professor asked, "What were you doing here for three years, if you didn't want to work in a hotel?"

"I don't want to build a career, I want to build my *own* chain of luxury apartments all over the world." When I answered, most people in the room laughed because they knew I did not have the finances. What they *didn't* know is just how badly I wanted this dream. I knew I had to keep pushing myself to achieve something in life, and this knowledge came from being a world-class athlete from a young age.

I was young, with dreams, passion for life, and achievements.

I was young, in a happy relationship, playing football, loved, and admired by many people!

For three years, I lived a wonderful life as I had my love, my friends, and my second team. I visited my family, had my own money, even bought my first car. I had time to reach my dreams.

In 2004, I was knocked down for the first time in my life! My dad was diagnosed with a brain tumor and expected to have six months to live. I packed my bags, got in my car, drove onto the ferry, and went back to mainland Greece. All I knew was I had to take care of my family, be with them. Hospitals, surgeries, doctors, and a trip to Cuba to get a new medicine that might save him—you name it, I did it.

Dad lived for 18 months. When he died, relatives told me I

was the one that had to stand tall, and remain strong to support my family.

It was then that I was scared for the first time in my life. I felt weak. My dad was always the strong one upon whom I could count on in any difficulty, but he was not there. The truth is, he trained me well. It's just that I had known he'd always be there in case I failed.

I'm still young! The youngest in the family! And then I realized that I had been prepared to take care of my family from the time I was nine.

Yes, I was scared, and at the same time determined! I had to be strong, had to take care of the family. And that's what I did.

I created my own cleaning company to provide jobs for my brothers and bought an apartment. My family supported me as I was supporting them. Life was going on, although the gap Dad's absence left was still huge. My mom, the hero she is, supported us emotionally, financially, and spiritually.

A year later, my brother John was diagnosed with multiple sclerosis. Mom prayed to God to change this. She asked me, "What are we going to do? What will you do if I can't be there to support your two brothers?"

Four words came out of my mouth. *I will be there.*

In a split second, the sibling balance changed. John and I, as the healthy ones, had made a commitment to support Sakis all our lives. Now Sakis and I agreed to support John.

In my lonely moments, I questioned my Creator: *What is it that you want from me? Why are you keeping me healthy when all my family is suffering?*

The next three years, I worked hard. I had no goals or dreams anymore; I wasn't seeking knowledge. I was living day to day with no purpose.

Suddenly, I had the chance to buy a piece of land overlooking the sea, and instantly my old dream came back to life. I knew I had to work hard for years to make the next step, but I knew, *This is a beginning!* An income property, something to support my family if I wasn't healthy enough to work.

The Greek economy soured and I struggled to sustain my business, pay my bills, and pay for my apartment and the land. Because I had created a good name for my company, I managed to survive. If I knew then all I know today about finances, that crisis wouldn't have affected me at all.

In 2011, I met my soul mate, Roula. Life changed instantly— *so* much happiness—and it brought out a different me. In October 2013, we became involved in a travel club. We shared the same goal—to travel and help others do the same.

It took just one event to change my goals, and the funny thing is I was a know-it-all—I didn't even want to go and had excuse after excuse. I will always thank my partners, George and Chris, for insisting and pushing us to be there. Eventually we said *yes.*

On the second day of the event, I suddenly realized *I* was the prisoner being portrayed on stage. I realized that no bars kept me doing what I was doing daily; all that I did wasn't related to what I truly desired in life. At that moment, I saw how cleverly the system imprisons most people, keeping us busy, making money to be spent on things we never really needed in the first place, just to pay our bills and barely survive. Eight hours a day, five days a week, 40 years of our lives, if we live that long!

Lord, I cried. I wish I had this information when my dad was still alive; he would have lived a better life, still short perhaps, but much better. Thank God I got this knowledge now. It's freedom I want, and I want it *now*!

I finally understood I needed to develop myself, I needed to grow—mentally, emotionally, spiritually, professionally, and financially. I needed personal development and growth.

My decision was made: I would work toward my freedom and show everyone how they can do the same. At that point, I had no idea how I would make this happen; I just knew I was determined to make it happen!

I finally found my purpose. I knew it. It filled my heart, my soul, my brain, my blood was pumping in my veins. I couldn't keep this information for myself. I needed to share it with the world. It was the love for humans that made this urgent to me. I couldn't wait to get back to Greece and start sharing the vision.

When you make a decision, things start happening for you! Your eyes can see things you couldn't see before. Your ears can hear things you couldn't hear before, you feel things you couldn't feel before.

My real journey began. I had a purpose in life. I now knew why I was born. I employed more people so I wouldn't work in my own company and I started enrolling like never before. The dream started working and I decided to sell my cleaning company to invest even more in myself and the training system.

There were so many times we got close to the next rank but didn't make it. *Why?* We never missed training, we were enrolling, went on DreamTrips; why wasn't it happening? Why couldn't people see the vision?

Even worse, I was struggling more financially. Five years went by, and we were experiencing a plateau, a long, long plateau. I had no income! I couldn't pay my bills, had no electricity at home, and people were pointing out my failures, my error in getting involved with network marketing and selling my business! I desperately needed answers.

Finally I asked the right questions:

*What can I learn from my choices so far?*

*What do I need to do differently?*

*How can I grow?*

*What am I missing?*

I realized I wasn't ready to go higher.

All I cared about was *me* and the recognition *I* could have. It was all me and my goals, my survival.

But I wanted to change! This wasn't truly me.

I thank God I never missed an event.

I thank God I kept on reading books.

I thank God I listened to audios daily.

If I hadn't, I would have given up!

Instead I talked with my love, my family, and my team, and told them I was moving to the United Kingdom to become a live-in caregiver. I'd pay my bills and loans and have enough for events and trips. It was the way to gain back my self-respect, and as a bonus, I would learn to better care for John, who was by then in a wheelchair.

It was the way to make me care again.

My family understood, and my mother gave me her blessing when I left: *"Child, open your wings and fly! All I want is for you to be happy."*

When I arrived in the United Kingdom, I was frightened as hell; I was out of my comfort zone, *way* out. Still, I was excited because I love adventures. From day one, I knew these people counted on me; they needed attention, a sense of security, companionship, and above all, love!

I had so much to give inside me; I'd just forgotten I had it. Their need unlocked my heart A sweet smile and simple *thank-you for all you do for me* from a 99-year-old lady at bedtime was more than enough to make me work even harder the next morning. Despite the countless times I woke during the night to reassure my clients everything was okay and they were safe. Despite the nights I slept on the armchair next to the bed so they would go to sleep, every morning I woke with the energy to make their lives better.

I was getting back on track financially.

When I became Caregiver of the Month, I was shocked and filled with joy, but felt even more responsibility, and realized the award taught me something important.

When you do everything possible for recognition, it won't last. When you do everything in your power to help others, recognition comes to stay! I put in heart and soul to provide the best care because they needed me, not caring about rewards or recognition. *Put love in what you do, in everything you do*, I said to myself. Lesson learned.

Everything was going so unexpectedly well, I even started thinking of building the luxury apartments again. I planned my first break, a DreamTrip with my friends, my team, and my love. Couldn't wait!

All that time, I was making dreams for two, plans for two, pushing myself to go further so I wouldn't disappoint my love, but I wasn't sharing them. I wanted to say everything in person. All that time, my mind was focused on everything except my relationship.

When we were ready to go, I discovered my love was already with someone else. I was devastated and wounded.

After the trip, I visited my family, showing up happy and strong, hiding my betrayal. I shared the caregiving skills I'd learned and they truly helped my wheelchair-bound brother.

My family gave me so much love during my visit, it gave me courage to keep going. I knew I needed to dream and plan again, this time for one—*me*.

When I arrived in England, the questions exploded in my mind:

What can I learn from this?

How can I become a better lover, a better friend?

What can I do different so this won't happen again?

Does God have something better in store for me?

Did all this happen to challenge my dreams?

I fell on my knees, praying to God to give me the answers, to show me the signs so I can follow the path I was born to follow, to help me become the best version of myself in *all* aspects in life.

And God answered.

A week later, I got the information I needed to start building my luxury apartments at the end of 2019.

Two weeks later, my brothers enrolled at the university and John was awarded extra financial support from the government.

A month later, I signed a contract to become Johnny Wimbrey's *Break Through* coauthor.

I see my dreams becoming reality one by one.

One emotion triggered this all, and I'm sure it will be the same until the end of my time. It's pretty obvious, isn't it?

**Love what you do and your life will be a masterpiece.**

Don't miss out on your life.

Get involved to evolve.

Day in and day out, work with yourself. It is never too soon, it is never too late to go after what you love.

Make each day the best it can be and focus on what you want to become.

Make the world wonder how it would be if you had not come this way by serving your purpose. It's really up to you, and you only.

# Biography

Christina Velidou was born and raised in Florina, Greece. She became a professional football player, representing her country at a very young age. She learned when you commit, work hard and stay focused, you can achieve everything.

Christina is fascinated by traveling and interacting with multiple cultures and people, and wants to help them all find their purpose in life.

## Contact Information:

Email: christinavelidou@gmail.com
Instagram: @christinavelidou
Facebook: Christina Velidou
Skype: Christina Velidou

# CHAPTER NINE

# Let Forgiveness Free You

## Kyonna F. Brown

Today, I am secure, bold, and some might say arrogant, but it's pure confidence. When I stopped blaming everyone else for my actions and faced reality—that *I* was responsible for what I did—my life changed forever. For me, the beginning of the process was forgiveness, something we all know and love to hate.

Forgiveness is the one free thing every one of us can choose to give to others, but really it's a life-changing gift we can give to ourselves. I finally began to understand forgiveness when I was sitting in a five-by-ten-foot jail cell and facing fifteen to thirty years of incarceration.

"How did I get here?" I wondered. "Hell, how do I get *out* of here?"

The cell provided me with the bare accommodations I needed for survival—and there weren't many. I had a bed, a toilet, some toilet paper, and a few toiletries. That was it. Once upon a time, I thought I needed all kinds of lavish things to live. But as I was learning fast, usually we have more than we need. I was all kinds of nervous. I did not know what to expect beyond the door of my cell. Murderers, drug dealers, gang members, and God only knows who else were out there. Sure, I was tough. I came from Trinidad, one of the worst neighborhoods in Washington, D.C., but was I a match for the people on the other side of my cell door? I had no clue.

The day I arrived, my questions weren't about to be answered. The entire jail was on lockdown because some inmates had figured out a way to travel through the jail's walls. I had a lot of alone time to think about why and how I got there. Most of the time, though, I slept. I told the guards I had allergies so I could get Benadryl; it knocked me out so I could sleep as much as possible. But when I was awake, I was angry, I cried, I wrote, and I cursed God. One day I finally asked Him why He had left me.

*You left me!* The voice reverberated in my head, so close it sounded just behind me.

From that moment on, I started to think about my journey, and I can remember it as if it were yesterday.

As a little girl, I was standoffish. My mom tried to do things with me and I did not want to be bothered. She even gave me a brother just so I could have companionship. I am a loner, still to this day. I can remember playing house in my bedroom at my grandparents' house—just me and my doll baby. No play father; no other children.

With my parents living the drug life of the 1980s, my elderly grandparents who did their best, and a brother who was doing his own thing, I got used to being alone. Have you ever felt alone when you were in an environment filled with people? That was me during elementary and junior high school. My low self-esteem and lack of self-confidence kept me under the radar. I had crushes on boys, but they never knew, and they walked past me as if I did not exist.

A side effect of my mother being incarcerated was that my brother and I were required to see a therapist, and I know I experienced the symptoms of depression at a young age. I did not share a lot in therapy because I believed I was the one who "had it together." I could not allow my weakness to be seen by others, not even a psychotherapist. Instead of talking about my problems, I ate my way to comfort. As a child, I also got comfort from my dogs, because they showed me love and compassion when no one else would.

When I was six years old, I began piano lessons and continued taking them until I was in junior high school. At the time, I thought I hated my lessons, but when I found out about marching band, I was drawn to the music and began to appreciate having had the opportunity to learn to read music. The band opened a whole new world for me.

When I was accepted into a high-school program that was miles away from my neighborhood, I knew I had the chance to be free. It was the first time I got a chance to recreate myself. Though I had a longer commute uptown, and I did not know anybody there, I knew I wanted to join the band at my new school. Being in the band was like a secret world inside of a world. It did not matter what you looked like, or if you were popular or not. I had the best times of my life in band. It was also when I was introduced to marijuana and the thrill of riding in stolen cars (we never got caught). It was also when I was introduced to writing. Band was the portal to both the good and the bad things in my life.

At this point, my mom was back in my life, though I did

not live with her, and my father was in and out, usually only seeing us when he was going through a drug spell because he wanted money for drugs or he took something else from my brother and me. It was impossible for us to keep anything with our father around. One moment our belongings were there, and the next moment they were gone, never to be seen again, sold for drug money. I did not like or trust my father. He was constantly lying to us and breaking promises. One of the times he hurt me the most was when he did not attend my cotillion. The other girls' dads were there, but not mine.

After my sophomore year, my mother had herself together. She was in school, working, and free of drugs and alcohol. She wanted her children back, and she said it had never been her intention for it to be for long when she signed the custody paperwork. Now she was ready to take us back, and I wanted to know what it would be like living with her. My father was still in the street life and I tried to duck him as much as I could. I loved my grandparents, but I was ready to explore the new. My brother believed my grandparents' house was his home. He was still angry with our mom; I just wanted to leave.

Leaving my entire life behind to live with my mom was exciting and scary. "Here I go again. It's time to recreate Kyonna," I thought. I was a little older and I felt like I would have more confidence walking into a new school. I was from the city—Washington, D.C.—and my mom lived in a rural area south of there. I was going to be popular because I had that tough "city girl" act to live up to.

Unfortunately, it did not work that way. I felt like a stranger in my new school and had to fit in all over again. I connected only with the outcasts—the students who were not popular.

The school band was disappointing. It just played classical music, which was not to my taste. I felt as if I was not smart enough to be in the school.

At my new school, I picked up with drugs and alcohol right where my mother left off. I had allergies and would pretend to have outbreaks, just to stay home. I did a lot of things to avoid dealing with the reality of being an overweight teenager. By that time, I weighed about 300 pounds.

When I reached my senior year, I was out of control. I started skipping school, staying out late, and smoking more marijuana than ever. By portraying that tough girl, as I had since arriving at the school, I became lost. I could not get the attention of the boys I was interested in, so I started dating girls. I was desperate for love, affection, and attention, and I found it. At that point in my life, I was being shown love by mostly female family members—my grandmothers and my mom—and men did not have a presence. That carried over into my relationships.

I enjoyed being sexual with females, but I knew I ultimately wanted to be with a man. I became so wrapped up in the lesbian lifestyle and the attention I received that I did not know how to escape it. In that world, it would not have been okay for me to be with both males and females. Bisexuality was looked down upon, and I did not want to lose the friends I did have, so I did not pursue relationships with males, though I did occasionally have phone conversations with them. Publicly, I was Kyonna the lesbian.

I did not have a lot of relationships; I was and still am a monogamous person. Emotionally, it was easier to be with a woman because women accepted me, weight and all. I continued to date women because it was what I knew.

One night when I was still in high school, I went out with friends and we had a lot of fun at the clubs. At the end of the evening when we went back to their place, I was anally raped by a male. My previous experience with women didn't prepare me for this in any way. I felt violated, as if my innocence had been taken from me by the rape, and I thought I would never be able to move on. I kept smelling the rapist and I kept on feeling the pain.

I didn't want to tell anyone about the rape and I didn't want to get in trouble because I was not supposed to have been at my friends' apartment. I felt it was my secret to keep, and just kept on going and wishing it would all disappear. I eventually buried it deep inside along with too many other experiences I'd had. I already hated men enough because of my dad. Through him, I had developed vengeance in my heart, and I wanted him to die. After being raped, my self-worth went even further downhill.

Fortunately, it was time for me to move on to the next chapter in my life—college.

Tuskegee University had admitted me and it was a wonderful opportunity—but I didn't believe I was smart enough to be there. I recreated myself again, but this time I formulated a monster. I don't think there was a time that I wasn't high at Tuskegee. I was high to escape myself.

I was even high when I took 15 Percocet tablets in an attempt to kill myself, and when I woke up because my suicide attempt had not been successful, I was angry. My friends at college knew how much I was partying, but no one else did. I didn't do the work I needed to and flunked out at the end of my first year.

After I flunked out, I went home and worked at fast food restaurants, but I couldn't wait to get off work and go out and party. I wanted to be high all the time.

Fortunately, a couple of months into my self-destructive summer, my mother and I had a conversation that changed my life forever. She told me she believed that I needed to get into the pet industry. Most of my past jobs outside of fast food had involved working with animals in some capacity or another. When my mother spoke, I listened. I went to an interview at a pet hospital for a veterinary technician position and was hired. The clinic taught me how to care for and groom pets and I got a slight confidence boost.

A month or so later, I met a woman almost my mom's age, and she became my reason to smile. All I ever wanted in life— love, money, and attention—she packaged and gave to me. We were going to get married. Before we did, we had a violent fight and I was almost choked to death by the woman I loved. Though I left, she said she was sorry and somehow I returned.

By that time, though, she had fallen on hard times, and she decided that robbing a store would give us the financial relief we needed. I agreed to help; we committed the crime—and yes, we were arrested.

In my jail cell, as I relived key moments of my life, I recognized a chain reaction of me being hurt and holding on to the pain. The hurt started with my dad, and I packed on layer upon layer upon layer. The hurt influenced how I behaved in relationships and how I reacted to my environment. My breakthrough was triggered by being locked up.

When we hide our emotions inside ourselves, they

eventually need to be released for us to function properly. Before the store robbery, I was free physically, but my mind was locked up in revenge and unforgiveness.

I served my time, and my four years in prison were anything but destructive. Working with a therapist allowed me to reveal my past, release my pain, and regain my confidence.

Today, I share the message of forgiveness with warriors who have lost their fight. I help them rediscover their hidden confidence, and that allows them to regain their authority.

Today, I have taken ownership of my life. I no longer play the blame game. I wrote out my master plan and I have stuck to my list of goals since my release. Part of owning my life is finally understanding that I am heterosexual, and my relationships with women were just part of my journey. More than a decade ago, after a tough break up with another woman, I found myself in an abandoned house. When I looked in a mirror. I couldn't even recognize myself. I realized I was tired of going back and forth with my emotions. I was upset with the way my life was going. It was as if every relationship I had buried me deeper in a hole.

At that moment, I remembered a friend inviting me to her church. It was a Sunday and I decided to go. During the service, I had an experience with God that changed my life and I have not looked back. I also have not thought about being in a relationship with another woman since then.

I am married now, and my husband and I have a six-year-old son. The life I share with them is not perfect, but it is filled with enormous love and joy. I'm happy, I'm loved, and I'm free—all because I forgave *me*.

No, I didn't hit it out of the park right away, but I kept

working at it. I allowed today to be a stepping stone for a greater tomorrow.

Forgiveness has freed me and it can free you. As a result of being free, I have been able to develop a relationship with my father, who is currently serving a life sentence in prison.

Don't let your past dictate your future. Allow your vision for greatness to determine your destination.

# Biography

Kyonna F. Brown is *The Forgiveness Expert.* She helps warrior women rediscover their inner confidence and regain their authority over their lives. As an inspirational speaker who has appeared on many stages, she uses her past experiences to inspire others and help them heal through forgiveness.

Brown believes her journey is blessed by God. Without His help, she would still be in the same troubled mental state, with her past dictating her present. Because she began dealing with the symptoms of depression at an early age, Brown now understands that her depression led to many things, including obesity, drug abuse, and, in her case, four years in prison.

Kyonna owns and operates Pooch Styles, a thriving pet grooming business in the greater Washington, D.C. area. Kyonna is a certified creative groomer and pet aesthetician. She is a backer of NeVetica, a revolutionary MLM company for pets.

She's also the author of several other books: *How to Care for the Pet I Love,* and *Blessed Hands: The Pathway to Forgiveness,* and co-author of *Breaking Free Forever: The Momentous Journey.* She hosts WBGR's *Forgiveness Friday,* a weekly internet radio show dedicated to dealing with life's issues and forgiveness. The show can be viewed on Facebook, Firestick, and Roku. She is a prison mentor with the Christian Mentoring and Transition Program and a field correspondent for *His Favor* Magazine.

She and her husband Charles have one son Jeremiah and three dogs.

# Contact Information:

Email: info@kyonnafbrown.com

Websites:

www.kyonnafbrown.com

www.poochstylespetgrooming.com

Facebook: @theforgivenessexpert

Instagram: @theforgivenessexpert

CHAPTER TEN

# Live Your Life—
# Don't Escape It!

### Brandon Fahrmeier

As a young boy growing up on a farm, I didn't think I was part of anything special or had anything special going for me. Looking back, I developed the gift of dreaming at a very young age when I ran around on the farm. We kids were encouraged to explore and allowed to play anywhere we wanted.

We went into the woods for hours, which to us seemed like days, weeks, and even longer. We built forts, tree houses, and acted out our dreams and our lives. Time was suspended when we stepped into this new world. This was the start of my journey of being a big dreamer and knowing that whatever I set my mind to, I could achieve.

Our parents always encouraged us to be entrepreneurial. I think I was about 10 years old when I bought my first steer for a 4-H project. I was responsible for that animal's care every day, and my steer probably lived better than I did most days. I'd get up early and feed him and take him to the barn. After school, I came straight home, headed to the barn, gave him a bath, and talked to him. We became best friends. The hard lesson of reality set in one day late summer when I needed to sell the animal who had become my friend.

Our farm was a business. Raising and selling animals was how we paid our bills. With tears running down my face, I walked my steer to the ring at the local auction to be sold for market. It was a hard lesson that I learned that day, but one that will stay with me for the rest of my life. Business is not emotional, but part of life. When you attach yourself to a business emotionally, then you act on emotion and can misguide your business.

Going through school, I always did average work, just sliding by, even in college. Though I was active in all social parts of school, I never really applied myself to my studies because I was always focused on work. I had two jobs through college; my parents helped but really didn't have the money to pay for all of my schooling. I had lots of help through scholarships the first couple of years, and when those ran out, I knew I didn't want to have a lot of student loans at the end of college, probably because I was taught not to rack up debt if you could help it.

Learning the difference between good debt and bad debt was taught to me very early in life. My parents were never frivolous with their spending, so I think that was always in the back of my mind.

College also taught me some great lessons. Having two jobs and going to class taught me to stay focused, because if I wasn't, I would fall behind on my classes very fast. Classes always seemed be the first to slide, because I was almost too good of an employee. I always worked overtime and was never late, and I never questioned what I was asked to do even when I didn't think it was the right way of doing it. My approach is if I have a way to do something better, I offer that suggestion.

My work ethic came from growing up on a farm, I guess. My dad always said if you're late, it shows disrespect for the person you are meeting, and it says you don't value their time. He was such a wise man. I learned so much from his lessons throughout the years.

Then one day, the switch suddenly flipped, though I am not sure even now which event or lesson caused me to change. I started climbing the ladder very fast at all my jobs. My mind had been expanded and I started being open to more.

After college, I became a school teacher and was never satisfied, though I loved teaching and expanding the minds of students to the possibilities that were out there. I had this burning desire to always do more, I really didn't know what, but I knew there had to be more in store for me!

Surely this was not all I was supposed to do in life, I wanted to explore the world. So, while I continued teaching, I launched a landscaping and greenhouse business; it had nothing to do with what I wanted, but my mind was limited to the possibilities of what I could do. I would teach school during the day and work on the business sometimes until one or two in the morning, and then do it all again the next day. Another lesson from my dad and grandfather: If you want more, just work harder than everyone else and you can have it.

But here is where I have learned a lot looking back: That is so true, but if you add working *smart* to that equation, you can amplify your success.

I ended up selling that business and moving back to my home to help with my grandfather who was suffering from Alzheimer's. I would not trade that time with him for anything.

About six months after my grandfather passed, I was approached to take a sales job working for Ball Horticulture, a company out of West Chicago, Illinois. I learned so much from my time there and was exposed to my first world travel.

My mind was expanded, a few more logs were put on the fire on my dream; I didn't even realize yet what was in store for me.

Working my sales territory in Eastern Ohio, I met some amazing customers who made wine in their basements; it intrigued me, and soon I thought it'd be a great idea to become a wine maker. My mind was expanded, I didn't even drink wine prior to meeting them. I jumped in feet first, making wine in my basement as I continued working full time at Ball. I was so involved in wine that I helped a friend make wine for the first time; they too loved the process and even ended up opening the Maize Valley Winery in Ohio. Every aspect of my life was enriched. I met and eventually married Mary, a single mom and psychiatrist. Mary is an amazing woman and the love of my life.

I started reading books like *Rich Dad, Poor Dad*, and the next natural step was to get started investing in real-estate. Within a couple of years, my wife dropped the bomb, *I want to raise kids around our parents; we should move back home!* What? I just got started in real-estate investing.

So, we moved home! I found a job working for MasterTag, a division of Master Products, traveling for a sales position; I had twenty-two states to cover. I know what you're thinking. I was married and at this time, my daughter was two years old, with another one on the way. This was no life for a father, but I could not see any way to continue the life to which we had grown accustomed without traveling.

I wanted more for my family but was torn by wanting to be a good father and be more available to our children. We made a logical (to us) conclusion that the best way to eventually do that would be to become an entrepreneur, doing something I loved with great potential. We made the leap of faith and opened a winery on our family farm! That was coming full circle, back to agriculture.

We were back but not satisfied; I still had a burning desire to have more. Mary and I were partners with my family on the winery and farm, I still had a job, my wife was a psychiatrist, and we were still waiting for it. We lived in a single-wide trailer and we were sacrificing everything on a personal level to focus on our businesses. Life was way out of balance; we actually had no life.

We never traveled other than work, never for pleasure, and then a guy walked into my life and presented an opportunity to us that at the time looked like a savings plan for travel. That is what I saw. I might even force myself to take some time off.

Nope; four years later, instead I was opening a second winery, Arcadian Moon, and going on my own with financial partners. We didn't even have enough money to purchase the property, but we had a dream, so Mary and I scraped together all our savings and secured the earnest money for the loan. We were $50,000 short of having enough to purchase the property, let alone getting the loan we planned on for opening a winery. We prayed and asked for 90-day closing so we could find the money, but banks and friends were tapped out.

I told Mary, "If it is in God's plan, it will happen."

Ten days prior to the closing, when we had no hope of finding the money but were still holding on to our dream and leap of faith, a friend walks in and says, "What's wrong?"

I guess it was written all over my face. So, I told her.

She said, "That's what I come to talk to you about." She had exactly the amount to invest that we needed to open. The dream became reality!

However, I had what I always dreamed of—golden hand cuffs! I now had a business that owned me; I even had investors. My wife and kids lived a life on one side of the wall and me on the other. I was working eighteen- to twenty-hour days and not even taking time for supper with the family. Luckily, I married an amazing woman. My wife is a saint! She holds our family together; without her we would have never made it this far.

Then, one night I was talking to a couple of ladies; I will be forever grateful for our conversation. I am still not sure why, but my life changed completely that night. That conversation gave me perspective. I was sick and tired of being sick and tired and didn't even know I was at the end of my rope.

I thought I loved what I did (actually, I did and still do), and that kept me from realizing how trapped I felt. The winery is my dream, but to *own* it, not to be owned *by* it. I realized I was a visionary, not the implementor, and now I needed to develop a plan. What's a plan? As you can tell from my story, I have never planned anything, I always just jumped and the safety net appeared. I was a dreamer. If I dreamed it, it happened, each time getting a little better. (On the outside, that was. My businesses had grown to a point that they owned me.)

I followed up and called the guy who introduced me to the travel idea, and asked, "Are you still doing this?"

He said, "Nope, well not actively," he answered. He gave me a phone number for my soon-to-be "mother in business," Deborah Brown, to whom I will be forever grateful for all the lessons she has taught me. She introduced me to my mentor, Byron Schrag, who has taken my mind and stretched it to reach places I didn't know existed. He had what I wanted and didn't know how to get—time and money. He did what he wanted and when he wanted to do it. I have become closer to God because of his guidance. The burning desire I have is coming to reality. Traveling the world and living the life as a "Lifestyle Entrepreneur" is my dream coming true.

Now my life has changed. I have been the guy with a Dream with a capital D, and that has carried me this far only by the grace of God. Now, with my mentors, I am a guy with a Dream and focusing on a plan to achieve it.

Look out! If you dream it, you can achieve it! God doesn't put dreams in the hearts of man so that you can just dream. He wants you to go get them. Don't go on a vacation to escape your life, go because it *is* your life!

# Biography

Brandon Fahrmeier earned a Bachelor of Science in Agriculture Education from the University of Missouri, Columbia, where he was a member of the Alpha Gamma Rho Fraternity. He taught at East Buchanan Schools in Gower, Missouri, then transferred to Hilliard Technical School in St. Joseph, Missouri. While still teaching, he started a greenhouse and landscaping company. After teaching, Brandon had several successful positions managing sales territories.

He currently resides in Higginsville, Missouri with his wife, Mary, and his three daughters, Carly, 13, Chesney, 8, and Chloe, 11, where they own a winery, brewery, and restaurant.

# Contact Information:

Website: inspirationalvisionary.com
Instagram:@inspirationalvisionary

# CHAPTER ELEVEN

# The Power of *The Ask*

## Anita Hawkins

*T*he *Ask* takes many forms. It is extremely important to our growth and development that as children, we all learn *The Ask* successfully. Whether children need extra help in school or need guidance as they learn how to tie their shoes, knowing how to ask for assistance is vital. For many of us, it is a skill we rely on many times a day as children, but for whatever reason, we somehow lose it as adults.

Knowing how to ask is important. As an adult, I can vividly recall my grandmother always told me, "The only stupid question is the one that goes unasked." I always believed that quote only applied when I was in school, because at home the rule was "be seen and not heard." Sometimes it seemed that as a child you didn't have the right to pose questions nor could you challenge an authority figure or elder, even when you knew they were dead wrong.

I didn't have any idea that asking could be as difficult or challenging as it has been for me. As a little girl, I was told not to ask anybody for anything outside my household. If I didn't have the money or couldn't afford something, I was taught to do without. I was taught that you don't share your business with other people and you make do with what you have. If you mess up, you either fix the situation or deal with the results. Asking for help from anyone was never an option.

Growing up, I was part of a middle class family, and we lived well. My father owned a used car dealership and worked at an oil refinery and my mother drove a city bus. My grandmother owned several booming businesses and was quite the socialite around town. We were the givers in our community, not the takers or receivers. As long as I can remember, I have been surrounded by takers—people who ask for money, for cars on loan, for money that is never intended to be paid back, and for contributions to every idea and initiative across the board.

What makes *The Ask* so easy for some but extremely difficult for others?

I did not realize until January 2018 that I indeed had a fear of asking. For years, I always said that I did not have a fear of anything but God. Until I headed up my own nonprofit, I really didn't consider the *Power of The Ask* and how often I would have to ask and beg for assistance and help, nor did I have a clue on how to even do it. What does it even look like to ask? Remember, my family were givers, not askers, and I was raised to believe that if you didn't have it or couldn't afford something, you didn't need it, so learning how to receive was a task.

As a teen mom I struggled for a few years because it was imperative that I extend no further embarrassment towards my family or anyone close to us. So, I did what I had to do to maintain my life. Though I bore the scarlet letter, I sustained academically knowing that one day I would eventually shine. Maintaining two part-time jobs my senior year in high school, I still grieved for the people that I loved the most because the separation felt like death. This was a crucial time in my life where I needed to be supported the most, but I truly didn't know how to ask.

In 2018, my life changed when I was asked by a supporter, "Why didn't you reach out for my assistance because you know very well I can do this with my eyes closed?"

I was stunned that she even asked me that question, and I had no answer because I honestly didn't know. A week later, the same question was posed by someone else, and yet again I couldn't give an answer. I went home and began to pray, asking God to reveal my *why*.

"Lord please make it clear to me as to why I don't ask for help," I prayed. "Am I afraid, and if so, why? Do I walk in fear of rejection or is this simply learned behavior?"

The Lord dropped the answer into my spirit within seconds.

Was this all that it took—just for me to *ask?* Whether it's in my day-to-day life or in my relationship with God, it's apparent that asking for help or guidance is where I have always faltered. Finally, I've learned just in the last year that asking for help adds strength, not weakness.

How am I just learning this when I'm more than 40 years old? Do I really carry around that much pride or *that* much fear?

Without having a college education, I have excelled at everything I ever set out to become—licensed cosmetologist, licensed builder, franchise owner, author, model, philanthropist, talent manager, and producer.

I pushed past adversity, naysayers, teen motherhood, life's challenges, and more, yet asking for help was something I shied away from and I didn't know why.

To be totally transparent, I can say I still carry the same feeling that asking for something is a sign of weakness, even when I know that *I*, much less others, need help. I have always been the bearer of burdens for those closest to me, including my mentees. I never wanted other teen moms to experience what I went through. I wanted to make certain that I could provide a safe space where asking for help would be easy because they could trust me and be totally vulnerable. It's extremely important that we all have a support system of people who believe in us because we all need help throughout our lives. It took me several years to realize why I adopted my way of giving and not taking.

I have honestly lived the life of both the *haves* and *have-nots*. I grew up wanting for nothing: having the opportunity to work alongside my grandmother, feeding the homeless, attending some of the city's most highlighted soirées, fundraisers, traveling the country, and being inducted into the National Association for the Advancement of Colored People when I was five years old.

Outside of his nine-to-five job, my father was a fisherman and he owned a 40-foot Bayliner, so weekends off were a treat: *Let's go fishing!* My closest friends even got to hit the road with us on some of our journeys. My dad said the same rule applied whether you were a man or woman: "Give a man a fish and you feed him for a day; teach a man to fish and you feed him for a lifetime."

There was pretty much nothing I wasn't exposed to. Daddy and Grandma played huge roles in my success before I ever knew it because I had lived my life looking at the surface of things versus looking deeper at the person I could become. The foundation was set, I believed I knew my purpose, but I didn't know how to free myself from a self-institutionalized state of mind.

At that point I embarked on a period of my life where I

dreaded waking up for the simple fact that I didn't know where I would lay my head the following day, not knowing how to ask for the things I needed because I had never been put in such a vulnerable position. How do I fix things and what type of support do I really need? Will people be open to helping me because the need is so great?

So much already had been taken away from the little girl inside of me at such a tender age that she figured just about everyone who entered into her life were the enemy and were only there to have their way with her.

So, building a wall made of steel was imperative because that was the only way Anita would survive. I went back to the grind of what I knew—school and helping others to smile by giving back. Though I didn't have much, this was my know-how.

Letting go of suffering, regret, fear, and pain is what I asked God while I was flat on my face asking why I didn't have an answer to the fear behind *The Ask*.

After years of living in a certain mindset, it began to feel as if I was bringing myself a lot of hurt and pain unconsciously by surrounding myself with needy people. Everyone had a need or a want. Was this the energy I put out through my philanthropic efforts or how I communicated to others that if you need me, I'm here for you? If this was the case, how could I alleviate this issue? Or could I simply turn back the hands of time to regain all things lost?

There were tons of questions that were running through my mind when God gave me my answer. After all, His word tells us:

*The Lord will open to you His good treasure, the heavens, to give the rain to your land in its season, and to bless all the work of your hand. You shall lend to many nations, but you shall not borrow.*

—**Deuteronomy** 28:12 (King James Version)

That is why interpretation and thorough studying are important. You hear folks quoting scripture, but most people don't get to the core of the Word and how to apply it. Deuteronomy 28:12 pertains to the blessing of rain to reap a good harvest of seeds sown. However, the only part I heard *was you will be the lender and not the borrower.* In other words, if there is need and you have the ability to help, you should help.

Learning how to say no to the people that I loved was a task, but when I said no, I was filled with guilt. How is it that I am so good at giving and lack the ability to receive?

*Dear God,* I prayed, *I need you to recreate my narrative and show me how to push the reset button.*

And just like that, He did.

I learned in that moment that I walked in fear of *The Ask* and why. Unlike most people who may carry a spirit of rejection, constantly worried about getting a quick *no* versus a slow *yes,* my worries and fears were caused by giving up control. I had a fear of relinquishing any part of my being to someone else's hands. Anytime I even considered asking someone for anything, it created an instant emotional trigger that caused me to reconsider.

In my mind, I'd hear the question: *What are you going to do for me?* I would immediately revert to a terrified five-year-old.

No one in my family knew I had been molested for years, beginning when I was just five years old. When I was a child, it became fixed in my brain that whenever I needed or wanted something, I had to give a piece of myself away in order to get it.

For more than thirty-five years, this fear kept me from accepting or requesting the help I'd needed so many times.

Now I coach young women who have been trafficked as

sex workers or who been the victim of domestic violence, They, too, have the right to ask without fear of losing what they value within themselves. My organization teaches that the givers *never* have the right to take it.

# Biography

Anita Hawkins is a model, author, philanthropist, and entrepreneur with a fierce determination to succeed at whatever she sets out to accomplish.

Earlier in her career as a model and spokesperson, Anita walked the runway for many high-profile fashion events including LA Fashion Week, New York Fashion Week, and Neiman Marcus, and appeared on the *Hollywood Divas* reality show.

Behind the scenes, Anita also owned a beauty salon, taught at a beauty college, and taught beauty etiquette. Many of these started as for-profit enterprises, but as Anita's career has grown, they have shifted from for-profit to charitable organizations

Currently, Anita is a talent manager with The Green Room Management in Los Angeles, and simultaneously is executive producer of a feature film, the creator and producer of HomePlate108, and is working on a television series being marketed to several networks.

In 2014, after self-publishing her first book, *The Storm After The Storm*, Anita launched Find One Reason to Smile, a 501(c)(3) non-profit corporation, which raises awareness for survivors of domestic abuse and sex trafficking. Anita has been dubbed *The Producer of Smiles* because of her efforts to reinvent the smiles of women whose teeth have been knocked out by their abusers.

She was awarded the President's Philanthropy Award during the Obama Administration.

Anita is married to retired Major League Baseball relief

pitcher LaTroy Hawkins, and they have two children, Dakari, 26, and Troi, 17.

Anita and LaTroy have donated more than $1 million to charities they support. Most recently, they donated a home to the national domestic violence organization, Women Called Moses, to serve as a safe home for women and children fleeing abuse.

# Contact Information:

Website: AnitaEHawkins.com
Website: FindOneReasonToSmile.org
Email: Findonereasontosmile@gmail.com
Facebook: Anita Hawkins
Instagram: @aehfashion @findonereasontosmile
Twitter: aehfashion

# CHAPTER TWELVE

# Go Forth and Break Through

## Steven Palmieri

Along the journey of personal development, having the good fortune of encountering positive influences one-by-one is a priceless gift to be cherished forever. I have been fortunate to have had such influences in my life, and now it is my turn to pay it forward and share my insight with you.

When Johnny Wimbrey offered me the opportunity to participate in this book along with Les Brown, Nik Halik, and the other co-authors, I knew this opportunity was a great honor that also came with tremendous responsibility. Because this book is not about any one of the co-authors alone, its impact comes from its amalgamation of ideas, stories, and cultures of people of almost every socioeconomic background across the world.

As Malcolm Gladwell observes in his book *Outliers*, culture and history can shape human behavior and entire populations can be predisposed to success or lack thereof. But the ideas and stories outlined in this book show that as individuals, we each have the ability to shatter through collective predispositions to forge our own individual pathways in life.

As for my contribution to this book, my hope for you is that my words find a special place with you and that you may be positively impacted just as I have been by the words and ideas of so many great people who have come before me.

My name is Steven Palmieri. I was born on March 13, 1980, in New Orleans, Louisiana. I currently reside near Dallas, Texas, and this is my breakthrough story:

# Early breakthrough influences

I grew up in an average middle-class family. I learned the value of hard work from my parents who tirelessly worked until retirement to provide for our family. I learned the value of networking from my brother. Practically his whole life he wanted to work for a railroad, and he successfully made his dream a reality by pursuing his passion, meeting people, and working those connections to help guide him to, and then through, a life-long career that he still maintains today.

I learned the value of discipline from school. Every day for 12 years, I dressed up in a khaki uniform and attended schools where I was held accountable for the outcome of my actions.

I learned the value of perseverance from my wife. She moved to the United States when she was young and taught herself English. She put herself through college and is currently pursuing her dream of being a journalist by interning with the Spanish TV station Univision.

When I was 24 years old and bright-eyed with enthusiasm, my brother convinced me to pack up my belongings and move to Dallas. Shortly after I moved, he handed me an article from *Inc.* magazine written by a guy named Keith Ferrazzi, an author I had not heard of previously. Titled *The 10 Secrets of a Master Networker*, the article laid out the concept of working to find the people who will leverage you up in society.

The ability to be consciously aware of whom you allow to influence you is a powerful breakthrough! When you begin to embrace this idea and start to replace negative influences with positive ones, you will have taken one of the most crucial steps to beginning the journey of transforming your life from what it is to what it should be.

# The breakthrough mindset

One of the reasons why this book is so special to me is because co-author Les Brown has inspired me. Anyone who listens to him has almost undoubtedly heard him cite an African proverb that says, "If there is no enemy within, the enemy outside can do you no harm." The most important breakthrough that one can experience is a mindset breakthrough.

The Charles Dickens' classic *A Tale of Two Cities* demonstrates this perfectly in its opening paragraph: "It was the best of times, it was the worst of times, it was the age of wisdom, it was the age of foolishness . . . we had everything before us, we had nothing before us . . ." If we take a moment to let this sink in, we will find striking parallels between those words and almost any scenario in our journey of life. It is our mindset that shapes our opinions of the situations we experience.

Many people are familiar with Proverbs 29:18 (KJV): "Where there is no vision, the people perish…" One day, I had the good fortune of being turned on to a book called *Think and Grow Rich* by Napoleon Hill. The entire book expands on this eight-word message from a personal success perspective. Hill's book hit me hard. If we have no vision of what our future should look like, then we are destined to fail; however, if we burn a laser-focused vision of our future into our mind, then we will be pulled like a powerful magnet toward this vision.

Discovering that professional development does not far exceed personal development was another breakthrough. In other words, a person's business is merely a reflection of that person in the mirror. If we are not where we want to be professionally, then we need to keep developing ourselves personally.

Additionally, being open to all of life's experiences is an essential component of the breakthrough mindset. In *The Art of Exceptional Living*, Jim Rohn says regarding life's experiences: "It's like dialing the numbers into the lock. You've got five or six numbers dialed into the lock, the lock still won't come open, but you don't need five or six more, you just need one more."

Think about this for a moment. YOU-JUST-NEED-ONE-MORE. All too often, people turn down the opportunity to participate in new life experiences. We all know the excuses. "I'm too tired." "There's no money in that." Or how about the classic, "I'm good." Well, this may be true. Maybe a person is "good." But wouldn't it be nice to be "better?" In fact, the better you become, then the more you can positively impact other people!

Being open to trying new things without regard for negative outcomes is a crucial component of the concept of "finding one more number to open up the lock" so you can break through it.

# Breakthrough perseverance and character

It is said that good judgment comes from experience and experience comes from bad judgment. Our failures are often our greatest educators. Steve Jobs sums this up nicely in his book *Apple Confidential 2.0* when he says, "I'm the only person I know who has lost a quarter of a billion dollars in one year . . . . It's very character-building." Whether you are on the scale of Steve Jobs or you are 15 years old and you lose twenty dollars and it is all you have, the experience is a big deal. Financial freefalls are painful no matter what the amount and these experiences mold our characters.

Personally, I experienced a painful hit in 2009 when the real estate market crashed. I had some rental properties that were mortgaged and I was unable to maintain them. Looking back, it seems like it happened overnight; one day I had great credit and access to financing, and the next day my credit was shot and I couldn't get a $300 credit card. In 2009 and 2010, I recall trying to restructure my debts in bankruptcy court but the tide was not in my favor and the rental homes were returned to the mortgage companies by the bankruptcy trustee. This life experience has provided me with insight that cannot be taught in school and it has helped forge my financial business that I run today.

I recall reading *Rich Dad Poor Dad* by Robert Kiyosaki before I purchased my first home. One thing from that book finally hit me hard. This book takes the position, contrary to popular belief, that your house is *not* an asset—rather, it should be considered a liability. Although technically a house *is* an asset, the *mortgage* attached to it is a liability. Add to the equation property taxes, insurance, and maintenance, and one can easily see that a home sucks up cash flow rather than providing cash flow. The upside is only the gamble on future appreciation. It was a breakthrough for me to consider that sometimes the counter-cultural way of looking at things may be better than the commonly accepted way.

# Happiness and financial freedom

What is it that drives us? Why do we do what we do each day? What makes us happy? These are questions that have eluded mankind since the beginning of time. Perhaps the answers to these questions are not supposed to be revealed to us. More than 200 years ago, the authors of America's Declaration of Independence described mankind's natural rights of "life, liberty, and the *pursuit* of happiness" (emphasis added). The authors believed men had the *right* to life and liberty, as well as the *right to pursue* happiness, but happiness was *not* guaranteed. Why would we have to *pursue* happiness while life and liberty do not require such pursuit?

Too often people seem to associate money with negative things. One day, while listening to *The Art of Exceptional Living* by Jim Rohn, my understanding of money was set on the right track. He mentions that more money does not make a person bad, rather, more money enables a person to be more of what he or she is already inclined to be. A bad person with more money can now be bad to more people. On the other hand, a nice person with more money can now be nice to more people.

For me, financial freedom is a huge "why" of what drives me. The pursuit of money at the expense of others is selfish while the pursuit of money at the service of others is legitimate ambition. Over my career, I have helped thousands of individuals and small businesses with taxes, bookkeeping, debt, and credit issues, and there is a huge sense of satisfaction in helping someone. The philosophy of Zig Ziglar rings true when he says that you will get all you want in life, if you help enough other people get what they want.

We live on an economic planet. Money is how we exchange value with other people for goods and services. If you do not want to work 40 hours a week for 40 years only to retire on 40% of your income, then the pursuit of financial freedom can be a great driving force for your actions.

# Go forth and break through!

The breakthrough for each of us usually is not one event, but rather a long chain of events and decisions performed in sequence over many years. Throughout this chapter, you have experienced some of the stories, ideas, and influences that have contributed to the shaping of my personal story.

Now, it is time for you to pick up from here and create your own story. What will you do with this newfound experience to go out and influence others in a positive way?

# Biography

Steven Palmieri grew up in New Orleans, Louisiana. In 2002, he graduated from the University of New Orleans with a degree in business management.

Palmieri has always had an entrepreneurial spirit. While a junior and senior in high school, he waited tables, and in college, he began selling cars. In 2004, at age 24, Palmieri moved to Dallas, Texas, and began working as an automobile dealership finance manager. During the next few years, he gained extensive knowledge in the finance arena and began dabbling in real estate investing.

In 2008, Palmieri started a business, Innovation Finances, that helps people with financial issues. His company has helped thousands of people and small businesses with CFO, credit, debt, bookkeeping, and tax matters. He loves to help entrepreneurs and small businesses get their financial house of cards in order so they can focus less on worrying about their finances and more on running their businesses.

Today, Palmieri resides near Dallas with his lovely wife, Juanita Palmieri.

Palmieri credits his parents, Michael and Patricia, his brother Christopher, and countless other people with helping him through the ups-and-downs of his breakthrough journey.

Steven would love to speak with you!

# Contact Information:

Email: Steven@StevenPalmieri.com

Website: www.StevenPalmieri.com

Disclaimer: Nothing in this chapter is: a) advice or assistance to help a consumer improve credit; b) tax advice; c) investment advice; or d) legal advice.

# CHAPTER THIRTEEN

# Challenge Yourself to be Greater

### Eugene Fair

As a young boy growing up in the early 80s in the small town of Mount Croghan, South Carolina, I quickly learned about responsibility and how to be a provider. My mother worked at a food packaging plant and my father serviced electrical power lines; they didn't have much money to provide for my three brothers, my sister, and me.

When I was only ten years old, my father was hurt on the job and had to have surgery on both shoulders. The injury put him out of work indefinitely and left my mother as sole breadwinner, trying to provide for the entire family with only her small salary.

My brothers and I knew we had to do what we could to help support my mother and provide for the family, so we went to work for our uncle. He owned a small construction company, building houses, barns, and small structures, and he treated us like men. My brothers and I got up at 4 a.m. during the summer when school was out and often worked until the sun went down. The money was really good—we were making a few hundred dollars a week and I wasn't even a teenager. In my mind, I thought I was about to become rich.

The extra money kept our family afloat and things slowly started to get better. As my father's condition improved, he was able to start doing small jobs here and there, like hauling metal scraps and cutting down trees for firewood and selling it to multiple families throughout the city. My brothers and I worked with him as much as we could during the times that we weren't working for our uncle's construction company.

One winter, my father built a small house for our dog so he would have somewhere to keep warm and not freeze to death. I know some of you might think to yourself, "Why is the dog outside?" Where I grew up, dogs were outside animals, and not allowed to be in the house. If our parents had caught us with the dog in the house, we would not have had a dog anymore.

When our neighbors saw the little dog house that my dad had built, they wanted one for their pets as well, and the word got out. More and more orders came in, to the point it was hard for him to keep up with the demand. Those dog houses led into building small barns and playhouses for kids. Things were starting to look up for us.

When I turned 15, I was hired at a local grocery store as a stocker, bagger, and butcher. I did it all. I was working full-time year-round, after school, and on the weekends. I had dreams of playing high school football, but that dream was cut short due to the need for me to continue to work after school to help provide for my family. I was really upset and didn't take it well when my father told me I couldn't play because I needed to work. After a while, I was able to deal with it because deep down, I did not want our family to continue to struggle.

I kept the job at the grocery store until I graduated from high school. Shortly after graduation, I was hired at a local metal plant for a higher salary, and after a few months, I moved out and got my own place. I started hanging with the wrong crowd and doing things that I shouldn't have done, and trying to make money the wrong way. I started to see some of my close friends going to jail and even getting killed. I developed an attitude of not caring anymore and found myself always getting into fights and even shot at multiple times.

My situation deteriorated, and soon I asked my parents if I could move back in with them. Being loving parents, they welcomed me home. At the time, they didn't know of my illegal activities and shady friends, but soon they started to catch on that a lot had changed with me.

My mom and dad always taught me to do the right thing and keep God first, and I never lost sight of that. Mom dragged us to church even when we didn't want to go and, to this day, I'm glad she did.

One Friday night when I was 18, I went to a church revival with my cousin and noticed a friend, Jimmy, sitting in the row directly in front of me. Midway through the service, the pastor stopped preaching and looked directly at Jimmy and me, and said, "I need to speak with you two at the end of service."

I thought, "Why does she want to speak with *us*?"

When the service ended, we went to the back of the church and sat down with her. The pastor said, "God has shown me a vision of your lives. I've seen that you're out in the streets fighting all the time and involved in illegal activities."

I looked at Jimmy, thinking, "Yeah, sure, right."

The pastor continued, "God has shown me another vision, and if you don't change your ways, I can see death in your future."

Me being me, I did not believe her, just as I did not believe in prophets. I believed she was just picking up on rumors she may have heard.

The next Saturday morning, one of my friends knocked on my door.

"Have you heard about Jimmy?" he asked.

"No, what happened now?"

My friend didn't beat around any bush. "Jimmy was shot at the club last night and he died."

Jimmy died exactly one week to the day from the time the pastor sat us down and spoke with us. I was in shock; all I could think was, "When is it *my* time? Am I next?"

At that moment, I knew I'd had enough and something in my life had to change.

Thinking of the constant lessons from my mom and dad and the situation I was in with my friends, I knew it was time to do something different. It was time to make a decision about my life. One afternoon at work, I took a moment while sitting down and quietly reviewed my life. I thought back on all the things that I had been through and what I was currently going through.

"When I get off work," I told myself, "I'm going to take a drive to Florence, South Carolina, to take the ASVAB (Armed Services Vocational Aptitude Battery) test to see if I can get into the military."

When I got off work, that is exactly what I did.

"How can I help you?" the recruiter asked when I arrived at the recruiting station.

"I would like to take the ASVAB test to see if I can join the Navy."

I took the test, and to my own surprise, I did really well.

"When would you like to leave for boot camp?" the recruiter asked me.

I looked into his eyes, and said seriously, "Tomorrow, if you will let me."

He chuckled for a minute, looked at me and saw how determined I was, but he couldn't do it. "The earliest I can ship you out is next week."

That next week, I saw a car pulling up in my driveway, and it was my recruiter coming to pick me up.

I went through boot camp in Great Lakes, Illinois, in January 2001, and reported to my first naval ship shortly after, which was homeported in Pascagoula, Mississippi.

I was shocked that everything had happened so fast. I was in a city that I'd never been to, there were new faces I had never seen, and I didn't know what to expect. I was never really nervous about serving, however. I was open to the challenge and wanted to see where it might lead me. After the ship processed me and finished my check-in, I was told that I would be assigned to "Deck Department."

"Okay. Now what is Deck Department?" I asked myself.

I was told that because I came in without a designated rating, I would be assigned to "Deck," and I quickly learn what "Deck" was all about—we're the "workhorses" of the ship. Our job was mainly to preserve the ship, e.g., needle gunning the decks, and painting the hull of the ship. I told one of my fellow shipmates that it seemed like hard labor and that I didn't join the Navy for that. He laughed hysterically.

While I was assigned to the Deck Department, I encountered racism. First it was from a Petty Officer First Class—a man who was supposed to be one of my leaders. He accused me of going through his things and stealing from him in the middle of the night in our sleeping quarters, but it was a lie. Then my own Chief, the man I reported directly to, told me in so many words that he didn't like black people; he told me to my face that he wanted to beat me up. I never let any of that break me and I kept moving forward trying to do the best that I could.

After six months in the Deck Department, I requested to cross over and become an Information Systems Technician (IT), which would be specializing in communications technology. I was approved to start working with the ITs and about a year later, I was able to leave the ship and go back to Great Lakes, Illinois, to attend IT "A" school for advanced technical training.

On the second or third day of "A" school, a new student joined the class. As I got to know her, I learned why she was late checking into class. Ebon'e drove the 925 miles from her last command in Norfolk, Virginia, to Great Lakes, Illinois, alone during the winter and her car had broken down. She had been stranded on the road with no phone, food, or cash, and no way to stay warm because her car wouldn't start.

She made her way to a nearby hotel to see if she could use their phone to call her last command for assistance, but she didn't get the assistance she needed and nothing was done on her behalf. A stranger standing nearby overheard what she was going through and offered money and help so that she could get to her destination.

After talking to Ebon'e and hearing her story, I fell madly in love with her. We both were coming out of bad relationships and, at first, she wasn't entertaining the thought of being with me at all. I was gently persistent, though. We started spending more time together as friends and one day she invited me to go to church with her. As we walked into the church, right before we took our seats, the usher who was seating us looked at me and said, "You make sure you take good care of her." We looked at each other and smiled. We believe that God spoke into both of our lives that day! About a year and a half later, she accepted my hand in marriage.

My wife was approaching her four-year mark in the Navy and faced a decision. Ebon'e contacted her detailer to see if she could get stationed somewhere close to me and was told that her option was Iceland. The detailer was not willing to negotiate with her, so Ebon'e decided not to re-enlist so that she could be closer to me.

Shortly after she left the Navy, she started her own business in the fashion world and began marketing handbags. She was doing a local fashion show in Virginia Beach, Virginia, and a scout for New York Fashion Week saw her material and admired it to the point that he invited her to present her line in the upcoming New York Fashion Week show. Things were taking off for her, and I was so proud of her following her dreams.

I continued with my time in the Navy and was promoted to the rank of Petty Officer Second Class in 2004. Things were going better for me. My wife and I enjoy meeting like-minded people who want to better themselves. Through some close friends of ours, we met a couple who were part of the multi-level marketing industry. They shared their story with us and we just fell in love with the opportunity to serve others and to provide the much-needed service that comes with it.

We were meeting new people every day but one couple really made an impact on us. This couple who was in our upline was none other than Coach Kelvin and Yvetta Collins, multi-million-dollar earners. Their training and mentorship really changed our lives for the better.

Ebon'e and I always told ourselves, if an opportunity presented itself and we felt it was of God, we would trust him and follow our hearts—and that was one of those moments.

Unfortunately, Coach Kelvin Collins passed away shortly after and it broke our hearts to hear the news. As with any business, different things happen for different reasons and you have to make a decision on the best way to move forward and we agreed it was our time to move on. During that time, I also advanced to the pay grade of Petty Officer First Class and decided to make the Navy my career.

In 2014, I advanced to the rank of Chief Petty Officer, the seventh-highest enlisted rank in the U.S. Navy. Soon after my promotion, I launched my own clothing company, which is now known as Custom Shirts Unlimited. We specialize in workout clothing and shirts for the military and by the grace of God, have been doing really well.

We all go through our own trials and tribulations in life and some may feel trapped. I'm here to tell you, if you are sick and tired of being sick and tired, and you are in that place in your life that you want to make a change but you are letting your past hold you down, sometimes *you just have to take the jump*. The time is *now* for you to take the leap of faith to better your situation. Don't let fear of the unknown keep you back. You don't have to know it all, because no one can want success for you more than you want it for yourself.

While you read this, if you know there's greatness in you and know that you should be doing more but you're stuck in your job, just ask this of yourself: *What motivates me to go to a job every day, knowing how much money I'm going to make, regardless of how many hours I put in? What's my driving force to work harder and harder even though I'm going to make the same amount of money. What's my motivation? Is this exciting to me?*

Next ask: *Will I be more excited to work in a profession where my potential earnings are unlimited?*

If the answer is *yes*, then ask yourself, *Am I putting forth the effort to change my situation?*

It's time to get uncomfortable being in that comfortable position you're in right now. Don't get too comfortable because of a fear of the unknown. If you never challenge yourself to be greater, you will always be average! Let "average" be a thing of the past; it is time for MORE and the time is NOW!!

**If I can do it, so can you!**

# Biography

Eugene Fair has been an active duty military service member in the U.S. Navy for 18 years and has the rank of Chief Petty Officer. He and Ebon'e, his beautiful wife of 14 years, have two daughters, Azariah, nine years old, and Siyana, who is seven.

Eugene is an entrepreneur who has been involved in several businesses including multi-level marketing. He currently owns a clothing company and is also a real estate investor. Eugene has led several speaking engagements on planning for the future and how to be successful.

Eugene and his family reside in Florida.

# Contact Information:

Email: TheEntrepreneurMindset247@gmail.com
FaceBook: @TheEntrepreneurMindset247
Instagram: @TheEntrepreneurMindset247
YouTube: The Entrepreneur Mindset
Twitter: @TEMindset247

# CHAPTER FOURTEEN

# Almost Believed Them

## Valencia Ivy

Nobody "raised" me. Every lesson I learned was through life experiences, and I wasn't taught by a parent or guardian. I'm not big on crybabies, and I don't have a helluva lot of empathy for adults who give up on opportunities that I never had.

Children are another matter. I have unlimited amounts of love and patience for children, perhaps because I never received any when I was a child.

On my seventh birthday, my older brother and I went into foster care and became wards of the state for the rest of our childhoods. We were the youngest of five children. My strongest memories begin in foster care; I read that our strongest memories come from periods of strong emotion, both pain and happiness, and I know that's true. My brother and I were placed in the same home with a picture-perfect family in a beautiful suburban neighborhood.

Immediately after our social worker left the house, that feeling of "what's next?" settled in. My brother's room was upstairs and I shared a room with one of the two older daughters, about nineteen. He and I quickly noticed the effort the family put into keeping the two of us separated at meals and while we were home. We could only speak on the walk to and from school—and he and I would talk about everything that was happening.

The daughter I roomed with was horrible, and I was suffering from her emotional and mental abuse. She frequently reminded me that I wasn't part of her real family, that my mom was a crackhead, and that my grandmother had given us away. She didn't stop there; she added insult to injury and wrote insulting things about me on pieces of paper over and over again. I don't have a clue as to why she was so cruel.

I was miserable, didn't try in school, and failed the second grade. My brother, who is my hero, felt the same way and masterminded a plan to have us removed from the home. He purposely broke rules—He went outside without permission, and stayed out until nearly midnight. Our foster parents were furious. I heard them arguing that night with each other but the next morning they were super nice and calm, and even allowed my brother and me to eat breakfast together for the first time.

When we got home from school, the social worker was back and our belongings were at the door. That was that for the perfect suburban family. I cried, because even though I was being abused, I had accepted it. The abusive behavior directed at me became normal and familiar, and as a child, you need the familiar.

Our next foster home was a different scenario—an older woman and her adopted son, who was my brother's age. I had a beautiful bedroom just for me and I got to see my big brother all the time. I was able to go outside and play and make friends on our block. I had a cake on my birthday, and at church I sang in the Sunshine Choir, and everything seemed perfect. It wasn't.

That was where the remainder of my innocence was chipped

away and I started learning (or not learning) my value. The adopted son was a very disturbed boy, and after six months he began molesting me sexually. At first, he would sneak in my room late, when everyone should have been in bed, and touch me inappropriately. As time passed, he became bolder and would do it whenever he thought no one was around or watching— always when my brother was gone.

Maria, a girl who previously was a foster child in the same house, came by to visit my foster mom. She asked me if the adopted son was touching me, and she said that was why she was removed from the home. Maria had told my foster mom about it when it was happening to her. She said my foster mother reacted quickly and jumped on her son, but he continued to do it, and one day, her social worker removed her from the house.

Maria told my brother that she thought the boy was touching me and my brother asked me about it. When I told him *yes*, I remember him crying in anger and frustration. I felt as if I should have lied to him and said *no*. I didn't want him upset with me and I didn't want to have to leave my first real family experience. I didn't know any better; I was just a child who wanted something normal and familiar.

After the beating my brother gave my molester, it was time for us to go, but this time we were headed back to live with family.

It's exciting when you're filled with thoughts of going home to live with your siblings, cousins, and an aunt. But not every guardian takes on the responsibility out of the kindness of their heart or because they actually love you and want the best for you. Sometimes they take you in for the money. That is when I realized that I had a cash value associated with my head. Crazy, I know but oh too real.

I lived with my aunt and her three daughters, and I thought it was normal in every family to fight till someone was hospitalized—literally. My first fight was with my cousins, I had to learn very quickly how to defend myself and I quickly learned I did it a little too well. My mother had the same skill, unfortunately. My guardian was filled with contempt for my mother—and I happened to look exactly like her.

One of the darker lessons I learned is that people will use you without caring how it will affect you later in life. Although I had been molested before, I didn't lose my virginity until I was eleven and living in my aunt's home. A member of the household bargained my innocence away to a much-older man.

My guardian didn't care what happened to me or anyone in the house, when we left, how long we were gone, who we invited into the house, or who stayed over. This is probably why I didn't bring many people around my children or into my home; even now I'm not big on house guests.

It's not surprising that I became pregnant at 13. I remember the day I told my aunt; her response was less than warm or encouraging.

"Look at you, throwing your life away. You're gonna be just like your mother; you will waste your life, too. You can't bring any babies into MY house, so you call your mother and tell her to come and get you."

I was officially a ward of the State of Illinois and if my mother came for me, she could have been jailed for kidnapping. But I called anyway.

My mother did come and get me, and I was happy. I had never had the experience of living with mom full-time *ever* because she was always in and out of prison. This was going to be different because Mom was married and her baby girl was having a baby.

I moved with my mom and stepfather to Ann Arbor, Michigan, right near the heart of the University of Michigan campus. The three of us were living in a one-room apartment, a tiny place, but we made it work. I didn't complain because I was with my mother, the woman I resembled, the woman who was constantly a celebrity in our family, but a mysterious, dangerous, taboo one.

My daughter was born and everything was going great; we even moved to a larger apartment. I thought things were looking up, I thought for a few months.

But when the holidays came around, I lost my mom once again to prison. She made some bad choices trying to provide for her family and it landed her back in prison for close to six years. That hurt. I was fourteen years old, with a five-month-old baby, and no direction. My stepfather had never raised any children and he was just as lost.

At this point I learned survival. There was a time we had no food in the house, no diapers, and no formula. My first born went through the struggle with me, because she was always on my hip. Always. It was no longer about me; it was about *her* and I had to make it happen. I had to make what seemed impossible possible. We were okay for a while but I needed guidance and help, so it was time to go back to Chicago.

I moved in with my older sister who was barely in her mid-20s. She did her best with the tools she had, though that wasn't much. We shared the same motherless experience with one big difference—she was raised by family members with love, and she had been *raised*. Although it was rocky and difficult, I was her baby sister and I know she wanted to protect me and take care of me and her niece as best she could.

Unfortunately, I had an ungrateful attitude. It was more

"You owe me," "What do you want from me?" and plain old "F___ off"—and had a strong dose of teenager. I felt as if I was an adult because I was a new mom, with a dose of "Becky Badass." When I went to live with my sister I was 15; and before hitting my sixteenth birthday, I was pregnant again, kicked out of school for fighting, and fighting with my sister about how to raise my daughter. I moved in with another slightly younger sister, and she became my legal guardian.

I never saw the inside of a school again. My education stopped at eighth grade. There were no high school dances, no proms, no football or basketball games, no anything. I was a stay-at-home mother/babysitter who, because of the children I had and the self-esteem I lacked, was a target for predators. The predator who I thought was my boyfriend later became the father of one of my children, but this predator was a provider— he picked up where the State of Illinois and my guardian faltered. It is easy to think that *at least you are loved by somebody* when it is not love at all.

When you're being used and manipulated as a sixteen-year-old girl, the mother of two children with one more on the way, things get hazy and unclear. I began to just walk through life, numb to everything I missed out on because I was convinced none of those things were intended for me. I learned how to provide for my babies very early on. I mastered a few skills— changing diapers, making formula, preparing quick meals, and last but not least, one that I'm not so proud of: how to make crack and sell it. That was a new me emerging, and although that last skill was very short lived, it never left my memory.

I am the child of a drug abuser who probably used drugs while pregnant with me, and have fragmented flashbacks of shelters or jail from when I was very small. I had always promised myself I wouldn't be anything like my mom. Her addiction and love of drugs kept her from being my mother, and that hurt.

When I turned 21, I was released from being a ward of the state of Illinois, but I had no education and no life skills. I was the mother of three children and clueless as to how to provide for my family.

I needed work and needed it fast. A friend of mine had a relative who worked for a jeweler who needed help, put in a good word for me, and BOOM, I had my first job. I was so happy I was working and living on my own. I earned enough to cover my bills and that was awesome. It was worth the crazy long commute, dragging my three kids along. We were up at 5 or 6 a.m. Monday through Friday. We went through cold winters standing at bus stops and having to catch two buses and a train just to drop my children at two different YMCAs and then continue on to get to work before 9 a.m.

The commute home was just as rough and cold, and sometimes we got home after 9 p.m.

"Momma, why don't we have a car?" my oldest daughter once asked me while we stood at the bus stop on a cold, nasty, slushy, day.

The words rang in my ears.

"Why *didn't* we have a car?" I thought.

I wanted a damn car.

I wanted that damn fancy bottle of perfume I saw in the big department store window.

Awakening my hunger for more was both good and bad. The new feeling made me step out of the shell I was living in, but I was naïve and allowed the wrong influence into my life. Let's call the influence "Satan." He was able to get into the head of a young woman who never knew her value, whom everyone dismissed.

It was a pretty easy task.

I took a chance to better my circumstances, one that most people should never do. It cost me close to five years' incarceration in a prison in Colombia, South America.

My life would never be the same.

It sounds strange, but a lot of positives came out of being in jail in Colombia. I learned to read, write, and speak fluent Spanish, holding full-blown conversations—and heated arguments—with other prisoners. I developed a few niche talents I still enjoy, such as carving.

Most positive experience was having my two youngest children in Colombia. Yes, my son was born in Bogotá County Hospital while an eighteen-year-old prison guard held my hand. My son was a blessing, born five years to the day after my daughter who died of SIDS when she was just three months old. My son become my cellmate and allowed me the luxury of a first-floor cell for just the two of us. He kept me company in prison for close to two years until I was released on parole and married his father.

When my next daughter was born, my husband and I were living in a middle-class area. It was nice, but money was tight, and I learned how to stretch a peso. While living there, I met some wonderful people and I am grateful for the experience.

If I had not learned how to endure and get through challenging times, I would never have known how to be present as a mother. I would never have appreciated having something nice. I would have never have had the intuition about questionable people and their intentions. I would never have had the courage to try something new and go after what I want. I learned that the decisions we make can be permanent so a person must be ready before making them.

I also learned that fear is a trait of the weak or confused. More importantly, I learned exactly how forgiving my God is because He keep leading me through dark places with a flashlight to help along the way.

Warmth and the ability to smile and laugh from the gut is a gift everyone has but most don't use—but it's very vital. It allowed me to come home to my older three daughters after being gone for five years and pick up where I left off. I was Momma again, thank God. My biggest fear had been not being accepted back into their lives.

My journey allowed me to be more cautious but kind and opened up the curious and wanderlust in me; I became a traveler very soon after. Adapting to other cultures and personalities is a talent I developed along the way.

If there's one thing I can share that you may remember, it's that people are going to disappoint you or count you out and sometimes you're going to find it hard to get through a day or a season, but you must allow your *struggles* to become your *strengths* and whatever motivates you to become your *engine*, your power. In my case, it's my children.

I'm sharing my story in the hope of giving some light and promise to any young girl who feels lost and turned away by family or by society. I want her to know this: *There are no obstacles too large or hurdles too tall to climb over. All I've been through and everything you are going through now builds character and strength, and in some cases, charisma. Never give up on yourself as others have.*

# Biography

Valencia Ivy was born February 7, 1977, in the south suburbs of Chicago. Since then, she has visited so many different countries that she can honestly say the world is her home. She's a success story, making it through challenges where most people would have folded, and she is a network marketer who's climbing the ranks.

Valencia is a mother of five—four daughters and a son—and she is a published author.

# Contact Information:

Email: ValenciaIvyv6@gmail.com
Facebook: Valencia.Ivy.1

# CHAPTER FIFTEEN

# Focus, Action and Hard Work

## Engels Valenzuela

The day I met my real mother, I was dressed in the best clothes I owned. I was five years old and had spent most of my childhood living in the Dominican Republic under the care of my aunt and grandmother. I grew up believing my aunt Brijida was my mother. My aunt told me my mother lived in New York and was finding a home for me, but I thought she was making up stories.

The day I met my real mother, I was excited to be going on a plane. At the airport, flight attendants approached my family and my cousin kneeled to my eye level to say goodbye. I realized I was about to be separated from my family and grew apprehensive. The flight attendants grabbed me and onto a plane I went. I was confused and scared.

When I landed in New York City, a woman approached me and hugged me.

"My son," she said. "I'm glad to see you."

I did not know what was happening.

Later, I learned the woman I had grown up calling *mami* truly was my aunt, and she didn't come to the airport to say goodbye because she couldn't handle the pain of letting me go.

My real mother had lived in New York City for a few years searching for a place we could all call home. "We" included my new half-sister, whom I never had met before, and my stepfather.

My aunts and grandmother shared many stories of how they grew up. The school system in the Dominican Republic required students to purchase their own materials, including textbooks. My grandparents didn't have the resources to buy pencils for each of their six children, and they broke pencils in half for them to share. My mother and her siblings used to fight for the half with the eraser. To study, the children had to find friends with textbooks.

My mother married my father, a Dominican in the U.S. Navy, at her father's insistence to better her family's economic well-being; she was not in love with him at the time.

My mother dreamed of her children being born in the United States and reaching their full potential in a land that offered many opportunities, and she made sure I was born on American soil. My father, however, returned to his home in the Dominican Republic, but my mother saw limited hope and opportunity there. They separated.

In the United States, my family was considered poor. However, comparing the easy access I had to food, clothing, warm water, and much more, made me realize my family in the Dominican Republic was much worse off. "Poor" had a different meaning in the Dominican Republic. People who were poor there were usually homeless. I saw myself as rich and I wanted my family there to feel the convenience and wealth I felt. I wanted them to have a better life.

I was in first grade and a teacher grabbed me by the shoulders and gently guided me to a line. The teacher spoke to me, but I had no idea what she was saying. I had a small problem, you see—I was a student in an English-speaking class, but I did not understand English.

My first English word was "nothing." I figured out the meaning of this word through my "English courses"; that is, animated shows like *Super Friends*, *Voltron*, *He-Man*, and *Heathcliff*. Initially, I could not understand the words but I could make sense of the storyline. My transition in New York City was less abrupt because I lived in a Dominican neighborhood—some grocery stores and restaurants only communicated in Spanish.

I eventually was switched to an all-Spanish-speaking class and made my way to bilingual and then English-speaking class by the fourth grade. English was never my best class, but I was great with math and science, perhaps because I didn't need good language skills for those subjects.

Acclimating to the culture in the United States was not my only challenge. I was still considered Dominican and there were expectations. Among my peers, I had to be active in sports, but my mother usually had no money to buy me equipment. I had to be presentable, which was difficult because the $10 needed for regular haircuts often was diverted for food. I did not exactly fit in with my peers, so I was picked on a lot. I was scrawny and not "cool." I was not smooth with my words in English or Spanish. My Spanish was good but upon coming to the United States, I had to focus on English. My English was bad because it's my second language. Nonetheless, I had to display a tough attitude whenever I could. The more I stood out, the more I got picked on.

At home, I also faced expectations. I was responsible for

doing all the grocery shopping, including buying and carrying home twenty pounds of rice with my 9-year-old body. I also purchased any cigarettes and beer my mother wanted. I helped my mother clean, including scrubbing floors on my hands and knees using only dish detergent and water. I also looked after my siblings while my mother was away running errands or attending church. At times, I asked my mother with frustration why I alone of all the children had all these responsibilities.

"You are the oldest," my mother replied.

I was not sure what to make of that.

One week, my fourth grade teacher was frustrated and made every student who did not complete the homework, stand in front of class, and explain to everyone why their homework was not done. When I first saw this, I told myself to avoid getting into this situation. Unfortunately, the day came when it was finally my turn to share with the class my reason/excuse. I couldn't look the class in the eyes and in my first sentence I started crying so hard I couldn't speak. My teacher got the gist anyway; she finally realized I was responsible for caring for my newborn brother.

"You are dumber than dirt," my two junior high school gym teachers told me and at first, I got angry. I finally learned if I stayed quiet, they would not pick on me.

Escaping my classmates was not as easy.

During gym, some of my classmates would steal other students' lunches. While the victim was playing basketball or dodgeball, some of the "cooler" kids would be taking pens, personal items, lunch, or whatever seemed interesting from the belongings of other students. I was against this, but I did not have the physical strength to speak up against the bigger and stronger classmates. In dodgeball, they came after me.

When I started retaliating against teachers in general and acting up, I became less of a target in dodgeball. That was an interesting coincidence.

On a day when I was misbehaving, I threw a paper ball at the head of my elderly seventh-grade math teacher. I missed by inches. I was disappointed about missing, but it turned out well.

The following week, the principal's office sent for me. Everyone assumed I was in trouble.

"This is good," I thought to myself. "I'm building respect."

I was not in trouble, however; instead, I was being rewarded. The math teacher whose head I had tried to hit with a paper ball fought passionately to get me out of her class and into the top class in the grade. I was being recognized for my math skills. This is my first realization that my strengths will get me farther into a better life and a real breakthrough for me. I was naturally great at math and other than the subject being easy for me, I did not take it as seriously. My abilities in math were my gateway to the top class in the school. Thereafter, there were new expectations. My overall grade-point average had to be at least an 85 percent, I had to choose and develop a talent, and I needed to do my best to represent the school on the math team. I moved into the Talent Academy and students in this section of the school had no choice but to choose and develop a talent: art, play an instrument, or sing.

Eleanor Roosevelt Junior High School held a chocolate sale contest every year, and when I was in seventh grade, the grand prize was a portable boombox. For music, my family relied on television or overhearing what the neighbors played, so I wanted the boombox badly.

My aunt Juanita helped me with the candy-selling venture.

For months, we spent afternoons knocking on each door within nearby high-rise apartment buildings. I won that year and again in eighth grade, when the prize was a portable TV. I liked that I did not need money to obtain these items.

These experiences led to two breakthroughs: I learned that through hard work and a focus on the end goal, I could achieve my objectives and dreams. Prior to this experience, I had a focus on money. I used to believe that because growing up with no money, I had a "poor" life. Though I desired a better standard of living, my life had not been "poor" at all. It had been filled with a wealth of learning.

When I was a freshman, I was in the Gateway Program at John F. Kennedy High School, and all my classes were either honors or advance placement. I was fortunate to be in a program with peers with a strong focus in academics and similar desires. Many of them also came from families enrolled in government assistance programs. My family received several types of government assistance and without that help, I am not sure what would have become of us.

By high school, I had four siblings, two half-sisters and two half-brothers, one a newborn baby with Down syndrome. I loved everyone in my family, including my new brother; however, my mother and I had a four-year fight about me caring for him as if I was the parent. I did not mind caring for him, but I considered waking in the middle of the night to feed him to be too great a burden. I told her it was not my responsibility to care for him, just as it had not been my decision to have a baby. I made the decision to focus on myself.

Taking a stand and focusing on myself was not easy and reflecting on it led to a few self-discoveries. My life had largely been determined by my mother and chance. This was probably the first time I made my own decision about my life instead of leaving it to my mother or chance. The other discovery was that for me to best assist my family financially, I first needed to focus on myself. In the Dominican culture, supporting family and being there when needed is a core belief. If I had focused then on supporting my family, it would have removed opportunities, so I did what I could to prioritize me and then family, and not the other way around.

During my sophomore year, however, one of my sisters reached into my stepfather's luggage and found seductive photos of a woman; he was cheating on my mother. As a result, my stepfather left the family. Things grew worse later that same year when our food stamps and other governmental benefits stopped. I was focused on my studies, performing well on the track team, and as a member of National Honor Society, but because my stepfather was no longer in the picture, I now also had to earn money and bring food home. As much I wanted to focus solely on my studies, my family needed me. I had to fulfill a role that was not of my own choosing.

I found a job at McDonald's and every day I reminded myself of my dream to become a professional. I would sometimes work till 11:59 p.m. on the activity most employees hated: collecting and taking garbage out to the mid-town pavement. If I had worked until midnight, it would have made me a legal liability because I was underage. I already was a liability, however. I stole food from the restaurant whenever I could. My family was hungry and I had to choose between feeling ashamed of my actions or helping my family.

Taking the McDonald job was my first meaningful decision, especially because it was against my mother's will. Wanting to attend university was now my desire and not because my mother pushed it on me. I had enough of those distractions and had a desire and focus on my goals and not because someone else insisted on me. I had focus and a dream: I wanted to attend a top-tier college outside of NYC, make a name for my family, and to help them get a better life. Having that clarity of dreams and goals made my path easier.

I arrived at Boston College via Greyhound with two suitcases, excited and immensely grateful to jumpstart my first year thanks to Advance Placement exams. I was appreciative of being on a scholarship covering 90 percent of my tuition and room/board.

In the year before I graduated, I realized I wanted a career in business, not computer science and premed as I originally thought. During my college years, I had coordinated entertainment events throughout Boston and Cambridge and had several related side businesses. I discovered that I liked orchestrating events and influencing people, and enjoyed making money. This was a breakthrough! My studies at Boston College had been based on my mother's desire to have a medical doctor in the family and my strong ability in computer science. When I was honest with myself, activities related to medicine were important but did not inspire me. I preferred reading books about entrepreneurship. I was more excited by working with a team and getting customers excited about a product or experience than anything else about it. I was lucky because many people leave this earth without knowing their true calling and I knew I was getting much warmer.

Before I graduated, I audited accounting and finance classes and read business journals and books. In 2003, I joined Jam'nastics, a Cambridge nonprofit organization, as director of Latin Department. Jam'nastics' goal was to get kids off the street and focused on their talents and education. My job there was simple—turn around a failing business and use the arts/sports of dance and gymnastics as a vehicle to build community, celebrate diversity, and promote positive change.

I did not know the answers but I knew I had the ability to figure them out. I quickly realized the problem was marketing. The key tasks I undertook included surveying existing students, developing email marketing campaigns, and increasing partnerships with other dance companies. My efforts led to increased attendance, which resulted in more classes and events with greater turnouts that expanded cashflow. The nonprofit then was able to expand its youth program and offer scholarships.

In 2005, I went to work for another nonprofit, World Monuments Fund, where the finance director gave me a chance to prove my abilities in accounting and finance, managing an international $25M budget as I took accounting night classes through New York University.

In 2008, I worked at the Small Business Development Center in Manhattan alongside professors and lawyers from Baruch Business School. I spent a year refining more than twenty business plans for entrepreneurs, raising debt capital for a few businesses, and constructing financial models and statements.

I recognized the need to continue growing, so in 2009, I began an MBA program at Ross School of Business, University of Michigan. I learned to value businesses, evaluate investment projects, develop and execute marketing campaigns, and diagnose and revamp strategy and operations. While attending Ross, I worked on a multimillion-dollar marketing project at Microsoft.

Since earning my MBA, I have worked at Intel, Amazon, and Apple and continued to enhance my skills with the long-term purpose of fixing and growing smaller businesses. I have developed my leadership skills and managed multimillion-dollar projects.

My long-term goal is to develop a turnaround entrepreneur management fund that fuses private equity and venture capital. A network of investors would supply the money for me to work with the founders of small businesses, entrepreneurs with good ideas who have plateaued and are underfunded, whose businesses need to be turned around so they can grow.

My childhood trip to NYC was devastating, yet it was the gateway to attending well-known universities and my subsequent career. My mother sacrificed much to help her children reach their potential and she passed that desire on to me. I love solving complex business problems and refining processes to realize the full potential of a business. Maintaining focus, taking action, and working hard are key life lessons that continue to guide my success.

# Biography

Rising from extremely humble beginnings through perseverance, focus, and hard work, Engels Valenzuela has worked at Fortune 50 companies like Apple, Amazon, and Intel. He has managed multi-million to multi-billion projects from demand and supply management to financial budgeting and reporting to launching numerous well-known products like Amazon Echo and MacBooks.

Engels' passion is in creating and growing value in businesses by solving complicated business problems.

He holds a Bachelor of Science from Boston College and a Master of Business Administration from University of Michigan.

His message is simple: *"Success is based on clear goals, focus and constant action."*

# Contact Information:

www.engelsvalenzuela.com

Email: engels@evalenzuela.com

LinkedIn: www.linkedin.com/engelsvalenzuela

# CHAPTER SIXTEEN

# Master the Basics, Become the Master

### Gert Suik
### and
### Karl-Martin Kruse

A *breakthrough* often is described as an *overnight success*— but that's not really true. *Overnight success* is another term that's often used incorrectly, because most people who are tagged as overnight successes began their climb up the ladder years or even decades earlier.

We define our breakthrough moments as the *decisions* we make. Yes, it's that easy: The moment you decide what you're going to do with your life, that you're going to pursue it no matter what, *that* is your breakthrough.

You might think you've already had your breakthrough moment, but have you? Have you really, *really* committed to it? If not, then we hope you will after you've read our chapter.

Gert: I had my defining moment when I was just a kid. I grew up hearing my mom grieve over how she felt about the sort of life she was providing for her children but how she feared moving away from our alcoholic father. Thankfully, she did move away, despite her fears. That gave me a powerful desire to pursue greatness, to show her that she gave us children love, *real* love, not something materialistic. I wanted to make sure she knew she had given me everything I needed to be able to create an abundant lifestyle for her, my siblings, and my own future family and me.

Believing my mother had given me what I needed to succeed gave me hope that I had it in me to succeed, but for a long time, I didn't know to do it. But knowing how is actually irrelevant. If you have enough belief, a work ethic, and you always continue to improve yourself, then life will throw everything you need in your path.

I've always had a passion for creating graphics: pictures, videos, 3D models—anything. I used to watch amazing travel videos and dream about creating something just like that. But I had no experience traveling. Fortunately, I was able to surround myself with people who did not know anything about creating content but had traveled around the world like crazy, so it was a fit.

Through my passion, I found people who were like-minded—people who wanted to pursue greatness, just as I wanted to do and just as we all should want to do. The people who surround you is one of the critical points of being able to go after your goals. As this book's celebrity co-author Johnny Wimbrey said several months ago at a training, "We're all born to be winners, but we're programmed to lose." It really is our choice whether we're going to allow our own success or not. Society tries to make us think small, but it's our call as to whether or not we're going to let our friends do the same.

The people you hang out with determine who you are. You

all know that but few actually think about the consequences that your surroundings bring. Your salary equals the average of your five best buddies' salaries—think about it. It's about right, isn't it? Your personality fits into the middle of the bell curve, too, right? Some of your friends are more negative and skeptical about everything, and then a couple of friends are a little more optimistic and open-minded than you are.

I guarantee this truth: *Changing the people who surround you will change you as well.*

If you hang out with successful people who have achieved what you want to achieve, you will learn from them. Maybe it won't happen in the first week or month, yet their presence in your life will influence your thoughts and actions.

Success in life works the same way. You don't have to ditch your current friends, just add some more successful friends and their additional energy to your life.

**Karl-Martin:** The breakthrough in my life came when I understood we have no control over the years passing by—it happens no matter what—and what matters is *how* you use every second of your time, what are you doing with your life, and who do you spend time with?

In Estonia we say :"Show me who are your five best friends and I will tell you who you are." At first when I heard that from my parents, I was thinking that is not right, but now I am so certain of this, and it applies to everything.

Three years ago, I was working as hard as two people—and getting paid for less than one—and I was open for new challenges. I always have been open for new challenges, but this time I was pretty much desperate because I wasn't happy, or fulfilled, and I was wasting my time.

The main three things I wanted were:

1. To know how to be a better person and develop myself as a human.
2. To travel around the world.
3. More income.

I had surrounded myself with people who also were at a dead end; we drank a lot of alcohol after work or on the weekends. My best days were when I was partying and drunk with my friends.

So one day, someone I hadn't seen for a while calls and asks me: "How are you? So, I see you have found your dream job, eh?"

I admitted, "Yeah, right, I don't like this job, I want to travel, do my own biz, and learn how to communicate better with people."

My friend said: "Oh really? Then we have to meet. I have a travel company which I just started." So we set an appointment.

Since that meeting, I have trained myself, helped people to another level, helping them come back on track when they have been off track, and mentoring them.

**Gert:** Be aware of your surroundings. Follow people who have what you want and start implementing what they are doing. If you have a mentor in your life, you're blessed to have his or her time. In the digital age, there's a new definition of the concept of mentors, what people call "being mentored." Nowadays, a mentor can be someone from YouTube, Facebook, or Instagram. The internet is loaded with influencers from all around the world. Find someone who speaks to you—someone you can relate to—and follow them.

People often rely on someone or something to motivate

them. Motivational videos, books, and quotes do help to inspire you to action, but the effects wash off eventually. To keep myself inspired, I do at least a little bit of personal development every day. If I'm not able to read a book, I listen to audios on my phone, or in my car. I hardly ever just listen to the radio if I'm alone in my car.

**Karl-Martin:** When I had my breakthrough, I started on a new way of living, a fulfilled way of living, having my dreams and hopes back thanks to my new friends. They helped me even though I had no experience in business, MLM, sales, communicating, or mind-set. They took care of me like a newborn, teaching me how to walk, talk, act, and dress for success.

I was a hard learner. What I mean by that is, I wasn't the sharpest pencil in the box; usually it took me five to ten times to understand what I had to do, so I was a tough one. Thankfully, my mentors were consistent with me.

There I was, starting to read books, which I hated when I was at school; in fact, I didn't read any books while I went to school and now I *like* reading books. The knowledge you get from books is priceless, and you pick up new knowledge every time you re-read a book. This is because as you grow, you obtain the knowledge that's important to you at that moment. I guess I've read some books five to ten times by now.

The best thing about self-development is that you can help others with theirs. One friend had problems with her work, income, and mindset, and she was somewhat depressed. We talked, and every time we spoke, she found answers to her problems. It wasn't that I was giving her answers, but I was asking the right questions. In the end, you need to ask *yourself* the right questions.

My friend told me, "Thank you for coming into my life and guiding me in this journey. I am so thankful because if I didn't get this help, I would've quit and moved back to the life I used to have." Then I knew that everything I did was for the greater cause. The feeling of helping someone who is in deeper trouble than you are is a blessing.

Since then, I've adopted the mission of helping as many people as I can. As Zig Ziglar said, "You can have everything in life you want, if you will just help other people get what they want."

**Gert**: Maybe you can relate to this: When my life has been challenging and difficult at different points, I've found myself actually pushing away my personal development. Logically, we know it's totally opposite from what we should do. Why do we think we should take time off from personal development if life becomes difficult? It's the very thing that keeps us going, yet we stop giving it to ourselves? I know people deserve and need to take breaks from responsibilities, but *don't* take a break from personal development.

Let's suppose you love going to the gym in the morning because it gets you going before you start your regular day. At some point when you take a day off, you decide to skip going to the gym, thereby bypassing the very thing that gets you going in the morning. Do you want to get yourself going only for work, or do you want to get yourself going for *life?* The best motivation for ourselves is our *why*, which I learned more in depth at the travel company where I work.

The burning desire within you, your "*why*," is what gives your life a certain meaning. Write it out, memorize it, remind yourself of it every day. It could be anything. For me, it was my mom and family. For you, it could be your children, your spouse, or something from your childhood. If your motivation is bigger than yourself, great!

Why do I say that? People disappoint *themselves* every day, but we hardly ever disappoint people we love. Make the people you love aware of your *"why."* Doing so will drive you even more. Most people complain and whine about their boss, the politics, economics, and so forth. Don't be selfish—*do* something about it. If you can't do it for yourself, then do it for your family, the ones you love, so they won't suffer as you do.

**Karl-Martin:** Your mindset is one of the most important things in life. I say this because if you know what you want, you will get it. I like the quote by Jim Rohn, "If you really want something, you will find a way. If you don't, you will find an excuse."

One time I put together a dream board with pictures of what I wanted to have, *everything*: a healthy relationship, a better body, a new phone, a skydiving jump, and owning my own apartment. I misplaced it, and a few months went by. When I found it again, I checked what I had put onto the dream board, and it was amazing: In six months, I had bought a new phone, gone skydiving, and bought my own apartment. This is just how powerful your mind is.

Think of your mind as a gigantic magnet, and if you want something, you can pull it closer to you; the bigger the object, the longer it takes to it pull it. If you want something small, like "I want somebody to make me laugh," it is a small order to fix so it will come in to your life quickly. If you have a bigger goal, it will likely take more time. The important thing is *you have to believe it will come to you*, the more passionate you are and the more energy you project, the faster your goal will come to you.

Every day we think about 50,000-70,000 separate thoughts,

and 70% of the thoughts are from yesterday. We're like broken CD players, playing the same thoughts over and over each day. Here's where the power of thinking and the law of attraction come into play: If we constantly think about the things we want and how we want to feel and repeat those thoughts every day, then 100% of the thoughts we have are the things we want in life. It's crucial to program yourself *every day*. If you don't program yourself, life will program you. Who knows what plans life has for us! This is *your* time to take control of *your* life and get the dreams *you* want to achieve!

**Gert:** Most of us fail when we reach the point where it's finally time to do something. Our mindset, beliefs, and personal development habits are not going to cut it if we're not willing to do the work. The law of attraction is one of the most powerful law in the universe. The law of attraction is the ability to attract into our lives whatever we are focusing on, whether it is positive or negative.

You might be a master of focusing on positive thoughts, and perhaps life is still gifting you most of the necessities in your life. But if you just decide to turn on the TV and have a sandwich, that's not going to cut it. If you look at the most successful people in the world, even those you believe live probably the life of leisure, in reality they're constantly working hard on whatever they are doing. Successful people don't work for the money or fame; it's for the love of the game.

It can be tough sometimes, but be excited about it, because after every decrease there will be an increase. I believe you should be excited about how difficult the tough times are, because the law of attraction works best when you feel your emotions in addition to your conscious thoughts. If you want to be an entrepreneur, have a beautiful home, travel the world, and have your ideal life, how does thinking about that make you *feel*? How would you *feel* if you already had achieved those things?

You also need to *think* like you already have achieved it all. Imagine being in your dream home with your family. Create yourself a Dream Board and Affirmation Cards and look at those things every day. Combine that inspiration with hard work, ethics, and discipline. Trust me when I say this—it works like magic. As Napoleon Hill, who wrote one of the best books about the law of attraction, said, "Whatever the mind of man can conceive and believe, it can achieve!" Be relentless with your dreams and never ever give up on them, because you never know what might have been just around the corner if you had not quit. Of course, it might be hard and uncomfortable at times, but remember, if it's uncomfortable you are doing the right thing.

Always be teachable. There are a lot of breakthrough stories in this book, and when you read some of the chapters, you might think, "I know that." No, you *don't* know *it* until you apply *it*. I am aware of the many tips in *Break Through*, but because I know something about them does not mean I have nothing more to learn. Your growth is only limited by your ability to learn more. Master the basics and you'll become the master. The wealthiest people on this planet constantly keep working on themselves and so should you. Be humble enough to acknowledge to yourself that there's always room to improve on everything.

**Gert and Karl-Martin:** It is our absolute joy to bring our breakthrough stories to you, because we know that by far we are not the best authors in this book. We are ambassadors of the *breakthrough*.

169

# Biography

Gert Suik and Karl-Martin Kruse are the Co-Founders of Nothing 2 Great, which promotes and encourages people to take action to turn their life from *nothing* to *great*. The company works to give people more hope, bring other peoples' dreams back to life, and share knowledge on the path of personal development.

Both men live in Tartu, Estonia. Gert grew up in a small village with an alcoholic father, a mom who earned minimum wage, and four siblings, all seven living in a one-bedroom house. He recalls the early years were not easy, but the whole family, especially his mother, gave him a lot more than financial security—they believed in him because of the good grades he earned in school. Their faith led him to pursue a life of greatness as a way to give back to his family.

While in high school, Gert had a job in construction and there he met Karl-Martin, though they did not become partners until later. As a business student, Gert received an offer to become a real estate agent; at only 24, he manages one of the biggest and most well-equipped shooting ranges in Europe.

Karl-Martin's childhood was more middle-class and comfortable; his entrepreneurial instincts were inspired by is mother's start-up abilities. He didn't do well in school, and an inability to sit still and focus led to a vocational educational program and dead-end jobs in construction and at McDonald's before he found his true path. In addition to his work with Nothing 2 Great, Karl-Martin now owns a car park with rentals, lends money to worthy causes and people, and manages his international travel business.

## Contact Information:

Website: www.nothing2great.com

Email: gert@nothing2great.com
Karlmartinkruse@gmail.com

Facebook: Gert.Suik
Karl-Martin Kruse

Instagram: karlmartin.kruse

# CHAPTER SEVENTEEN

# Seven Killer Rules

## Steven Phillippe

D o you enjoy waking up every morning living the average life, with an average bank account, and most importantly, an average mindset? If you do, please skip my chapter because it holds nothing of value for you.

If you want to live above what you ever thought possible, to leave a legacy, and most importantly, have the desire to learn how to perform at your peak and win, then please read on. If any of these qualities resonated with you, then get ready to experience the true essence of maximizing your mindset and providing yourself with the confidence to follow your heart and chase what's rightfully yours.

Before I became immersed in personal development, I was working 60 to 70 hours a week and I was going to school full-time. Attending classes and doing homework was like having another job. I had no time for anything and I was financially broke. The reason why I was working so hard is because work was all I knew—it was all I had seen my parents do. My mother had been working in the pharmaceutical industry for about six years and my father had been one of the top performers at Disney for fifteen straight years. Life was great! We went on vacation after vacation and created so many memories that would never be taken away from us.

But what *was* taken from us blindsided us all.

My father was laid off from his job and two months later, my mother also was laid off. That was the first time in my 19 years that I've ever seen my father with tears in his eyes.

"Guys, let's pray because I don't know how much longer we're going to have the house," my father said.

At that moment, I realized I had to manage my life differently because the definition of insanity is doing the same thing repeatedly while expecting a different result.

What my parents didn't realize is that a *job* can come and go at any point in time, but an acquired *skill set* always will stay with you wherever you go. Which brings me to my *Seven Killer Rules:*

## Rule Number 1

*Jobs are designed to pay the bills while a skill set is designed to get you anything that you want out of life.*

At this point in my life I said, "God, show me a way out. There has to be a way. I'm willing to do whatever it takes." Through chance, I reconnected with a high school friend, Dre who had gone from being an average student in high school to traveling the world and driving his dream car—a BMW—and one that was all paid for. I wanted to visit him so that I could learn how he had done it, but he was in New York City at the time and I didn't have the money to fly out and meet with him. I continued to pray for a big change in my life.

I went to the gym to let off stress and as soon as I arrived, I was shocked and delighted to see that same friend from high school was there, so I quickly approached him.

"How's everything? How's your family?" Dre asked.

"I don't care about any questions right now other than what is it that you do for a living?" I responded and he laughed.

"I don't show everyone what I do because people say they want more out of life, but often they're not willing to do what it takes to win at the highest level," Dre said.

## Rule Number 2

*Don't immediately reject opportunities about which you have no real knowledge. Sometimes, learning about good or bad opportunities can lead you toward better and bigger things.*

I quickly stopped him from speaking.

"People aren't really motivated; that's true. But I am," I told Dre.

"Let's meet back up after midnight, if you are serious." he said.

I believe he was testing me to see how hungry I was for information, knowing that I had work the next morning. We met at 1 a.m. and he spoke for an hour nonstop about personal development. Some of the things he opened my eyes to were amazing.

By 2 a.m., I was driving to his house to collect audios and books he offered me, and I started reading and learning before I went to bed. I read *Think and Grow Rich* by Napoleon Hill and I've never finished a book so quickly in my life. I finished it that same night because I was excited for change. After reading that book, I became the equivalent of a drug addict, except my drug of choice was personal development.

"What's the best advice you can give me personally since you have been immersed in personal development for years now?" I asked my friend.

"Develop your mind for twelve months straight," Dre told me.

## Rule Number 3

*The only way to break poor habits is to master new habits.*

"Steven, most people only listen to personal development for a couple of days, weeks, or months. What separates me from the pack is that I've been listening to personal development for five years straight. Be here a year from now still studying personal development and you will automatically began to open up the flood gates when it comes to making money," Dre advised.

My friend and I became business partners. Through him, I was able to gain access to multi-million-dollar earners. Where I came from, having access to that kind of power was unheard of. I was finally in a place that mentally felt like home for me. Who wouldn't want to be surrounded by a whole circle full of great talent? People like Johnny Wimbrey, Robert Kiyosaki, Matt Morris, Dr. David Pietsch, Shaquille O'Neal, Rudy Ruettiger, Jordan Belfort, Julio Acosta, Sashin Govender, Germaine Lewis and the list went on and on.

Having access to some of the biggest gurus on the planet allowed me to unlock a skill that has completely changed my life—the art of tonality—the ability to manipulate the tone of your voice in such a way that it almost seems hypnotic. Mastering tonality allows you to say things without actually saying the words, to persuade nearly every human being on the planet, and to infer anything at any point and time through tonality alone. Master tonality and you will be classified as an expert in your craft, an authority figure. Most importantly, mastering tonality provides the ability to build instant rapport effortlessly.

My mentors always told me to observe what the masses do and do the opposite. In my first year of studying tonality, I was able to accumulate more than seven hundred sales, with three months of training and nine months of selling on the phones. Between my two different sources of income in sales, I went from negative $427 to $80,000 in revenue that first year.

## Rule Number 4

*Don't join a business if your primary goal is to make money.*

That sounds kind of crazy, doesn't it? But it's not. Joining a business to make money will not get you paid. Join a business to have access to the people to which you currently don't have access. *It's just that simple.* Without being open-minded to business opportunities, it's practically impossible to gain access to the sources that will help you develop the skills you need in order to be successful. You can't see anything at all if you don't have access. It's a closed door waiting to be opened.

I can say with complete confidence that without jumping into a business opportunity that I knew absolutely nothing about, I wouldn't have come across the heavy hitters of the sales industry, especially Jordan Belfort and Germaine Lewis. Without that leap of faith, it would have been impossible to have the proper connections. These connections led me to the right people who taught me a skill that changed my entire life forever.

## Rule Number 5

*Get good at something worth being good at.*

Mastering a skill is not the only puzzle piece you have to solve. Knowing what skills to master is also vital to your success. I'm going to give you the raw truth because it's exactly what you need to hear. *Most people who are talented, intelligent, with a strong work ethic are still broke.*

Why? The reason they're broke is because they are too focused on learning skills that will get them an achievement to hang on the wall rather than developing the skills to create financial freedom. I'll make it really simple for you—don't become the Einstein of spelling bees; be the Einstein of sales. My mentor once said, either you're selling something or you're working for someone who does.

It does not matter what field, space, or niche in which you're involved; sales is a universal language that has no barriers or discrimination, and offers plenty of income to go around and claim.

As a matter of fact, I have some challenges for you.

I challenge everyone reading this chapter to master the art of tonality and still manage to remain broke a year from now.

I challenge you to become unconsciously competent using that skill.

I challenge you to learn tonality or any important sales skill and not have commas on every check you receive.

I challenge you to lose sleep until you're certified and incorporating sales into a way of life.

## **Rule Number 6**

*You have to be a little selfish to be successful.*

I heard Johnny Wimbrey say that once, and I couldn't agree more, because at the end of the day it's hard to free other people if you don't have your own freedom. What you focus on expands. Focus on *your* abilities, goals, legacy, finances, ambitions, desires, family, business, motivation, and your will to win. When you learn to win, you will automatically attract other people into your life who also have the desire to win. In turn, that will lead to more connections and give you the qualifications to lead others.

Don't feel ashamed if you're putting yourself first over others because putting yourself first is necessary to win at the highest level and help the people around you. It's no secret. Look at this list of greats and ask yourself how much time they invested in themselves before they were able to help others: Michael Jordan, Kobe Bryant, Muhammad Ali, Floyd Mayweather, Tiger Woods, Serena Williams, Gary Vaynerchuk, Jordan Belfort, Johnny Wimbrey and so on.

Become great and the people around you will began to achieve even greater things.

## Rule Number 7

*Develop the Mamba Mentality.*

*"Growing up, I wasn't the biggest or strongest. When my teammates who were better than me were out partying, I stayed in because I knew it would give me an edge. You just can't underestimate the power of showing up every single day and doing the work. If you want to be a champion, you have to have the champion mentality, Mamba Mentality."*

—Kobe Bryant

As the great Kobe Bryant has said, the Mamba Mentality is a way of life. Put simply, there may be smarter individuals out there with a better set of skills, performance, and resumé than you. At the end of the day, none of that matters. I've seen plenty of times where the students of this game we call life surpass their teachers, where the mentee becomes the mentor. Its okay to be outperformed; it's not okay to be outworked. If you never had or lose the confidence to press on and chase your dreams, it's simply because you haven't developed that killer instinct.

I use the Mamba Mentality in everyday life situations. Every day you're competing for championships. The only championship that will ever matter is the championship of self-gratitude—knowing you did everything you could possibly do to fulfill the desires you thought were only possible in your dreams. If you can remember just one thing from this chapter, remember: *Any skill can be mastered as long as the power of your mind is willing to allow it.*

You can take control of your thoughts or let your thoughts control you.

# Biography

A published author, Steven Phillippe is and was ranked in his company's Top 10 nationally in phone sales in his first year and was the youngest person in his company's history to ever hit the Top 10 in sales.

Phillippe came from humble beginnings, growing up in the projects of Orlando, Florida. He recalls walking home from school, hearing gunshots on every corner, and wondering if the bullet meant for him was hiding in the next block.

Now Phillippe drives a beautiful M-package sports, 4 series BMW. He has been on 20 vacations in the last few years and teaches others how to sell on the phone by helping them create dynamic sales scripts.

# Contact Information:

steven_phillippe@yahoo.com

Instagram: Steven_phillippe

Facebook: https://www.facebook.com/stevenphillippe81

# CHAPTER EIGHTEEN

# Escape the Ordinary

## Nik Halik

As a child, you used to dream. Your mind wasn't shackled by logic, false beliefs, or societal limitations. Everything was possible, and the world was wondrous and magical. Then, as you aged, you started developing false and limiting beliefs about yourself and the world around you. You started buying into societal programming. When people told you something wasn't possible, you believed them. When your peers chose jobs and careers based on their own internal limitations, you followed suit. You started thinking more "responsibly" and "sensibly." And in this process, the flame of your dreams died down to mere embers, and in some cases may have been entirely extinguished.

My invitation to you is to breathe life into your dreams again. Cast off the shackles of your false beliefs and societal programming. Realize the vast majority of your limitations are only in your mind.

What would you do if money was no longer the primary reason for doing or not doing something? What grand adventures would you live? What noble causes would you champion? What great feats would you accomplish?

I was born with a poor biological template. I developed chronic allergies, debilitating asthma, and I was nearsighted. I was medically confined to my bedroom for the first decade of my life. When I was eight years old, a traveling salesman knocked on our front door in Port Melbourne, Australia, and sold my non-English speaking Greek immigrant parents a set of the Encyclopedia Britannica. That set turned out to be one of the greatest influences on my life. It was the spark and secret kindling that set my imagination on fire. My imagination had stretched my mind, and it would never retract to its original dimensions.

I read the encyclopedia constantly and, without my parents knowing, I'd take it to bed with me. I'd shine a flashlight under the sheets, flick the pages of a volume through to a subject that fascinated me, and read until I nodded off to sleep. Sometimes I'd stay awake past midnight, dreaming about the things I was going to pursue in life, and imagining the world that was out there waiting for me.

Growing up, an inspirational character for me was the comic book adventurer named Tintin. Tintin was living the "never grow up" dream, and I traveled the world through his pages, taking in every exotic detail. I read and reread Tintin books in our school library, daydreaming about his magical life. In his various adventures he was a pilot, space explorer, mountain climber, and deep-sea diver. He also climbed the mountains of Nepal, rescued African slaves, battled pirates, and dived down to the deepest abyss of the ocean to explore shipwrecks.

When I reflect on the adventures of Tintin, I realize my

childhood dreams have come true. Many times, in the course of my adventures, I've been in some far-flung destination and had a weird feeling of déjà vu—a Tintin flashback. I was fascinated by space travel. Growing up, I was glued to the TV watching the United States and Russian launches.

Space travel was the big deal then. All this adventure fueled my desire to get in a rocket ship and go myself.

The encyclopedia, the lure of space travel, and the Tintin adventures opened up all the things I wanted to accomplish. I sat down and wrote my highest aspirations in life.

# Writing the Script of My Life

I drafted my own screenplay of goals. I was the actor, the producer, and the director. Here I am as an eight-year-old, with my list of ten life goals. Pretty ambitious. Dreaming and thinking big. That list has fueled my life. Since writing down that list at age eight, I've accomplished almost everything on the list. I have two major goals remaining: rocketing to a space station orbiting 250 miles above the Earth and walking on the moon. Even those goals are within my reach.

# My Adventures

I became the first flight-qualified, certified civilian astronaut from Australia, and was a backup astronaut for the TMA 13 NASA/Russian space mission. I remain in mission allocation status for a future space flight to the International Space Station.

For a few years, I lived in Moscow and graduated from the Yuri Gagarin Cosmonaut Training Center in Star City. During the Communist era, Soviet cosmonauts were quietly chosen, groomed, and trained behind a veil of secrecy.

My life has been filled with extreme adventures. I have visited over 152 countries. I have trekked with the Tuareg Bedouins across the Sahara Desert. I broke the sound barrier in a modified Russian MIG 25 supersonic interceptor jet traveling at almost Mach 3.2 (2,170 mph, 3,470 kmh) and viewed the curvature of the earth. My rock band performed and toured with big names like Bon Jovi and Deep Purple. I dived down five miles deep in a pressurized biosphere to have lunch on the bow of the shipwreck RMS Titanic in the North Atlantic Ocean.

I have climbed the highest peaks of five continents, including the mighty Mt. Aconcagua in the Andes. I have two more peaks to summit on my attempt to become one of a handful of climbers in history who have climbed the Seven Summits—the highest mountains of all seven of the world's continents. I did a Navy Seals HALO skydive jump with oxygen, above the summit of Mt. Everest in Nepal at over 30,000 feet, on my most recent birthday. I have rappelled into the heart of the most active volcanoes in the world. I have storm-chased tornadoes in the Midwest and hurricanes across the Atlantic Ocean.

I even negotiated with the former deposed dictator of Egypt to spend a night in the nearly 5,000-year-old Cheops Pyramid in Giza, Egypt. I spent the night alone in the King's Chamber of the pyramid and slept in the sarcophagus in total darkness—the very same sarcophagus that Napoleon Bonaparte, Alexander the Great, Herodotus, Sir Isaac Newton, and other giants of history had slept in. Media outlets dubbed me the "Thrillionaire."

*"Don't be an extra in your own movie"*
—Bob Proctor

# My Worldwide Business

During the last two decades, my companies have impacted more than one million people in fifty-seven countries. I deliver keynote speeches and facilitate entrepreneurial training courses around the world. I even get the opportunity to speak in remote locations most foreigners would simply never visit. Just recently, I spoke in the communist "hermit kingdom" of North Korea and taught geography to a classroom of teenagers about to graduate. I have conducted an entrepreneurial mastermind seminar to more than 750 investors and business owners in Tehran, Iran.

*Do not go where the path may lead, go instead where there is no path and leave a trail.*

—Ralph Waldo Emerson

# It's Time to Live Your Dreams

My adventurous life did not happen because I was born into wealth. Lacking a wealthy friend such as Tintin's Captain Haddock, I realized that if I wanted to become an adventurer like Tintin, I would need to develop multiple pillars of income in order to afford such a lifestyle. I wasn't born rich—but I was born rich in human potential. My life by design was never coincidental or lucky. I have merely acted out the script I created for my life—a screenplay I wrote as a young child. My manifested reality was the result of every decision made in my life. I did have medical issues earlier in my childhood, but I refused to be held captive by them. I was forced to clear any obstacles that threatened to obstruct my path of self-discovery.

I'm no more special than anyone else. I've simply set my sights on big goals and have never stopped working to achieve them. There's nothing stopping you from doing the same. You may not care about traveling or anything else I've done. I don't share my life experiences with you because I think you should care about anything I've accomplished, but rather to simply inspire you to live your own version of the ideal life.

There is no shortage of adventures to live and thrills to be experienced. You may want to live on the beach and surf every day. Perhaps you want to go on an epic RV trip. Your dream could be to do frequent humanitarian trips to developing countries. Maybe you just want to spend more time with your family or simply have the leisure time to read more.

Whatever it is for you, go after it. Don't let anyone tell you it's impossible; don't let anything stop you. Life is the greatest show on earth. Ensure you have front-row seats. You have an abundance of opportunities that people in the past could not even have dreamed of. Eliminate all excuses from your mind and vocabulary. Cut off the pessimists and haters in your life. Surround yourself with inspirational people, and immerse yourself in inspirational material. Do whatever it takes to escape the trap of the ordinary. Because I can promise you this:

It is so worth it.

*"Start by doing what's necessary; then do what's possible; and suddenly you are doing the impossible"*

**—St. Francis of Assisi**

# Biography

Nik Halik, The Thrillionaire® Entrepreneurial Alchemist, Civilian Astronaut, Extreme Adventurer, Keynote Speaker is the founder and chief executive officer of Financial Freedom Institute, Lifestyle Revolution, and 5 Day Weekend®. He became a multimillionaire and amassed great wealth through investments in property, business, and the financial markets. Nik's group of companies have financially educated and life coached more than 1 million clients in 57 countries. Nik generates passive income, building recurring subscription businesses, investing in tech startups, and multi-family apartment complexes. He is currently an angel investor and strategic adviser for several tech start-ups in the United States.

Halik has traveled to more than 150 countries, dived to the wreck of RMS Titanic to have lunch on the bow, been active as a mountaineer on some of the world's highest peaks, performed a high-altitude low-opening (HALO) skydive above the summit of Mt. Everest in the Himalayas, climbed into the crater of an exploding erupting volcano (1,700 degrees F) for an overnight sleepover, and just recently, entered North Korea to expose a sweatshop factory operating illegally for an American conglomerate.

He was the back-up astronaut for the NASA / Russian Soyuz TMA-13 flight to the International Space Station in 2008. He remains in mission allocation status for a future flight to Earth's only manned outpost in orbit—the International Space Station with Russia.

# Contact Information:

www.FollowNik.com

# CHAPTER NINETEEN

# Begin Your Life!
# Again!

## Michael Starr

I magine having $500,000 laying around in cash and various accounts, but not being able to get credit from any banks! That was my life when I was 26 years old. I was moving fast toward earning my first million dollars and getting ready to buy a house—for cash—because no banks would lend me the money.

Just 90 days later, it was all gone. I was heavily in debt and believed my life was over.

That was my life as a professional gambler and bookmaker in Australia.

From a young age, I had an appetite for risk. I was brought up around the greyhound racetracks because my dad, Arthur, was a licensed on-course bookmaker in the 1970s and 1980s. Being around my dad's profession exposed me to the concept of the fast dollar at an early age. Seeing thousands of dollars pour in and out of a bookie bag was just a regular thing to me; it was my *normal*.

Let's take a step back in time. I grew up in Sydney, Australia, in a traditional Greek family. My parents individually migrated from Greece when they were young, met in Australia, and I

**193**

was their first born. Our family grew over time and I had two younger sisters, Joanne and Anna, to look after as we grew up.

One of my earliest memories was my first day in preschool. When I said I grew up in a traditional Greek home in Australia, I meant we only spoke Greek at home. Everyone at school spoke English, so this was to become the first of many obstacles I would face in my life.

Growing up and going to school in the 70s and 80s in Australia was an interesting time. Most other kids, especially from European decent, had long last names, but mine was Starr. So, where you would normally think that the European kids with the long names would be the ones to get picked on, I was the outsider who was picked on.

My school years were not the most pleasant. I was a capable student with good grades and was always headed for a higher education. Every year, I was the youngest in my grade, so I was always the shortest. This may have been the reason I copped a lot of abuse, both mental and physical, especially in the high school years. During one period, it was so bad I made new friends in different parts of the school grounds to hide from the bullies.

There were times I would come home with bruises and had to lie to my mother so she wouldn't worry. I was too scared to tell anyone about what was going on—not the teachers and not my parents. As a result, over the years my self-esteem and confidence were chipped away. I lived every day wanting desperately to get out of an abusive situation but believing I had nowhere to turn.

At the end of tenth grade when I was not yet even 16 years old, I was offered a job in a bank. That was my way out, my freedom, but I had to convince my parents. I begged and made all types of promises, and they allowed me to leave school and go to work.

My life had just begun!

Australia is one of the few countries where you can still be a registered bookie—someone who sets odds and accepts bets on horse and greyhound races at the actual race tracks. Because my father was a licensed bookmaker, I was able to hang around the racetracks, and when I was 16, he received special approval to allow me to work for him as a bookmaker's clerk.

The banking job was great; because of my work ethic, I was promoted through the positions fast. I also worked two to three nights per week with my dad at the greyhound races for some extra cash. Unconsciously, I was being programmed to have a very large appetite for risk. You see, all I ever saw in the bank were large amounts of cash and transactions. All I ever saw at home was cash before and after the races along with talk of how many thousands of dollars were won or lost in the space of a few hours. I was becoming immune to the real value of the dollar.

As soon as I turned 18, I started wagering my own stakes on the tracks, and won regularly. Working all week to be handed the same amount of money I could earn on a single wager seemed like a waste of time, so I quickly put the concept of working for a boss on a nine-to-five schedule to rest.

After I left the bank, my dad insisted I come to work in the family auto repair business and I had to abide by his rules at my age, especially while still living at home. Eighteen months later, Dad sold me his share of the business, so by the time I was 20, I was in a partnership with my Uncle Chris—a relationship we continued for 10 years.

At 25, I became one of the youngest licensed bookmakers

in Australia. It was one of the most exciting times of my life! Learning the profession from my father at a young age, working in the bank, the years of being a bookmaker's clerk, and the years of wagering on my own, all set me up perfectly for this role. Becoming a licensed bookmaker was my BIG ticket. My life had just begun again, and things started to move really fast. I was moving quickly through the ranks, making a big name for myself, and being approved for a horse license, as well as greyhounds, was a dream come true. My father was also very proud and that felt good as well.

As a bookie, I could not apply for a home loan to buy a house. There was no regular salary to show the lender because profits and losses on a single day can be more than someone's annual income. The only way to buy one was to pay in cash, so I was gearing up to buy my first three-bedroom brick home for $190,000 (U.S.). The money was there and I had plenty more left over with which to keep working.

But what happens to a 26-year-old who hasn't faced any financial adversity and has undergone zero personal development? When things are going well for a bookie, it's just like something you see in the movies. You have the big young bookmaker, the high-profile wagering and betting duels, the high roller membership cards in the casinos, the big car, and the bundles of cash in the sock drawer at home. At some point, the ego takes over and greed kicks into overdrive. I lived the high life and had zero respect for money. Now add the fact that money is totally devalued on a race track, and I had all of the ingredients needed for a recipe for personal disaster.

One night after the races, I was dropping off one of my clerks before heading home. As I pulled over to let him out, someone opened my car door. Towering over me was a big man wearing a ski mask and holding a large knife that he pressed up against my throat. The robber turned my car off and took the keys. I was totally pinned. I looked in the rear vision mirror and a second robber had my clerk pinned in the back seat.

"Hand it over. I know you've got it on you," I heard him say. I couldn't believe I was being held up.

During the course of our lives, we make many choices and decisions. When you look back, you can see the chain of events after a particular choice or decision and whether it may have been a good one or not. That day I had made a choice. That choice was to take all the cash with me so that I could bank it the next day instead of using the armored truck that transported bookies' cash from racetrack to racetrack. I had more than $30,000 (U.S.) in my pockets and it was supposed to go toward my new home. Instead, I was handing it over bundle by bundle to the individual robbing me.

Nobody was hurt in the holdup, but this was the beginning of the end of my bookmaking career.

Over the next ninety days, I became totally reckless. I made ridiculous mistakes trying to "chase" the losses incurred in the robbery. Looking back, it must have triggered something in me. Maybe anger, maybe a larger ego—I don't know. What I do know is that I completely lost everything I had. The cash, the car, the bookie's license—all of it—and I was heavily in debt.

Everything I had worked for was gone except my share in the auto repair workshop, so I humbled myself and went back to fixing cars, which was extremely hard for me to do. I did manage to stay involved in the racing industry one day per week—Saturdays—just in case I got a lucky break.

Being open minded, I was always looking out for any type of opportunity to get me back in the game. About three years later, someone knocked on my workshop door and talked to me about saving money on my phone bill. This was another choice I had to make. Do I tell him to go away as I'm too busy, or do I give him a chance? I decided he was only doing his best to make a living, so I listened to what he had to say.

Well, he got his pen out, showed me how I could save 30% on my phone bill, and said he wasn't going to charge me for his services because he would receive a commission plus a residual commission payment every month I paid my bill. I was so impressed with the business model and how he earned income that I decided to investigate. What piqued my interest was the concept that I could earn a residual income for the business I wrote. Your customers *saved* money and you *made* money—what a concept! Within nine months, the 25-year-old family auto repair business was history and I was working in the telecommunications industry.

My life had begun again.

Early in 2001, I borrowed my parents' garage and used it to house my tiny telecommunications business firm. I was working hard to build a client base and regular income was coming in, debts were being paid, and my residual income was slowly building. I was starting to get back on track financially.

In 2004, I met Jules, whom I asked to help me with my tiny operation. Jules would later become my best friend, and further down the road, she became my wife. Things were going well, and Jules believed that within 12 months we would have our own office.

What Jules said actually happened! Within 12 months, we had bought out a smaller telecom company, moved to a proper office, and I was making a comeback. As my confidence grew, so did my desire to go back to the racing industry. It's in the blood, I guess. I had to prove to myself that I could make a comeback no matter what, but this time not as a bookie, but on the other side of the fence as a professional gambler. So, from Monday to Friday, I was the "phone guy" and every Saturday I was the "racing guy."

Despite the challenges, late nights, and my working all day every Saturday, Jules always supported me. She was my rock and still is to this day. Jules introduced me to the idea of personal development. We attended a weekend self-help seminar, which I didn't totally understand at the time, but I did enjoy it. I even read a couple of self-help books, which was a new concept to me because it wasn't something discussed in my social circles.

Jules and I were married and, in 2011, Jules stopped working to have our little boy, Athan. With another member in the family to look after, I started working even harder. In fact, I was working a solid ninety hours per week and rarely had a break.

A few years later, I received a very unusual call from a total stranger, Ivan, a young man from South Australia. He asked me all sorts of questions about my business model, how it worked, and how I started the company. It seemed suspicious and I thought he was going to open a competing business. This was another decision I made; I could have ended the conversation right there or been open minded. I decided he was clearly a go-getter, just like I had been at his age, so we talked for quite a while. We struck up a partnership and looked to grow the business nationally. Unfortunately, that didn't go quite as planned, but a great friendship formed and we kept in regular contact.

In July 2014, Ivan introduced me to a business concept that would change my life.

I was supposed to attend a two-day business and personal

development event with our new company, but to be honest, I wasn't going to go. I was working ninety hours per week and had no time, and my ego also had kicked in, saying "I know all this stuff!" Thankfully, Jules convinced me to go.

My idea was to turn up for half of Saturday and sneak out, but after the first ninety minutes, I was totally blown away! I met ordinary people from all walks of life with different backgrounds and nothing in common who were living the extraordinary lives they had created. I saw a glimpse of what could be possible for me and my family. It was a vision I've had from a young age, but I had been driving the wrong vehicles.

When I was finally surrounded by the *right* people—who would help me—instead of the *wrong* people—who just wanted to take advantage of me—I had my defining moment, my BREAKTHROUGH! It was like being struck by a bolt of lightning, and I knew right then what I needed to do to make my life better.

By the end of the weekend, I made a decision that changed the course of my life and the life of my family. I completely cut all ties with the racing industry. After more than twenty-five years without missing a Saturday (that's one thousand and three hundred Saturdays for anyone who is counting), tens of millions of dollars in turnover, and not being able to walk on a racetrack in my home state without being recognized, it was all gone in an instant! I looked back and finally saw the anxiety, the stress, and the dread, and I realized I did not want it any more. I saw myself buried under the burden of it all, and I was not happy.

As soon as I made the decision, I felt a huge weight had been lifted off my shoulders. At that moment, I realized I had been walking through life and looking ahead to the future with a giant dark cloud surrounding my whole life. In an instant, it was gone.

I felt totally free with a very bright future.

Jules has supported every choice I'd made since we met, but I know she was quite relieved for me to be out of that business. What that taught me is that my grief and my burdens had been hers as well, and when I took that out of my life, it went out of her life as well.

Looking back at the choices I'd made from the age of 16 forward, everything that happened brought me to this point. The wins, the losses, the struggles—but I never ever gave up!.

The challenges that are put in front of you sometimes are a test or a message. Learn from them and keep moving forward no matter what. It's never too late to learn or try something new, to develop yourself personally, to "have a go," as we say in Australia. Your age, background, and level of education are all irrelevant if you just stay positive, open minded, and put in some effort.

At the age of 44, my life had begun!

Again!

# Biography

Michael Starr is the founder and CEO of Logicall Communications. Born and raised in Sydney, Australia, he has worked as a bank officer, licensed on-course bookmaker, and auto repair shop owner.

Currently, Starr is a leader and trainer in the network marketing profession.

He and his beautiful wife, Jules, have one son, Athan, age 8.

Michael is also a mentor and coach to many people around the world, helping them create more freedom in their lives so they can make better choices and take more adventures. He loves traveling the world, trying new experiences, making new friends, and creating memories with his family.

Michael is also available for personal coaching.

# Contact Information:

Email: michael@michaelstarr.com.au
Website: www.michaelstarr.com.au
Instagram: michaelstarr88
Facebook: michaelstarr88

# CHAPTER TWENTY

# Beyond Devastation

### Regina Diann

Imagine living the life of your dreams, having your deepest and fondest desires fulfilled, only to have your world shattered to the point where some fragments no longer exist. Your past, your present, your future all seem for naught and hopeless.

I have faced many despairing situations, some of which would have taken most people out, until one almost took *me* out. It's not just my story but very possibly your story as well. Your devastation could look totally different but the process of walking through it and getting to the other side is the same hard work. If you haven't faced such challenges in your life, allow this to be a strategic tactical battle plan to empower and transform you to your next breakthrough.

We have a tendency to go to great lengths to either create the life of our dreams or to live a life designed with a certain outcome in mind. My dream was to have and experience unconditional, everlasting, passionate love with my spouse. I hoped to have intelligent, fun-loving children who would be world changers and impact those around them for the better. I aspired to a life of freedom and abundance. I wanted to establish wealth that could be passed on to future generations. The only thing better than imagining our dream life is actually living it.

# My Back Story

After being part of the first graduating class of electrical engineers at Alabama A&M University, I was hired by IBM—one of the top companies in the world at the time. Getting hired was by itself a great victory. I got to negotiate a starting salary that paid me more than what my parents ever had earned in their lives. IBM moved me across the country to Texas. Thirteen months later, I purchased my first home. A couple of years later, I was recruited by Texas Instruments (TI) and received a significant salary increase to join their team.

When I was 28, I married my soul mate, Edward. We had common values, goals, and similar life objectives. Four years later, my heart's capacity to love increased to massive proportions with the birth of my daughter, Eden. And just when I thought there was no way I could love anyone more, my son, Edward Jr., arrived three years later and proved me wrong.

Four days after delivering my daughter by caesarean section, we had to stay an extra day to monitor her. On Thursday morning, April 3rd, my mother called to check on Eden and shared with me that he had been awake all night listening to a rattle in her throat. Knowing that she had not been feeling well, I encouraged her to get checked out. What she was describing to me just did not sound right.

Later that evening, I received a call that my mother had collapsed. She was on her way to the hospital when it happened. Medical personnel were working to resuscitate her. Sitting in my hospital bed, I grabbed the blueberry muffin on the counter and said to myself, "This can't be. She went to the doctor today. She is only 54 years old. She is going to pull through this. Her baby just had her own first baby and needs her."

The phone rang again and the impossibility became a reality: my mother was gone. The coroner later ruled the cause of her death was a pulmonary embolism that caused my mom to go into cardiac arrest. At 31 years old, I was the matriarch of our family. Everything in me went numb. I truly had believed my mom would be right by my side to support, lead, and guide me as I hit the major milestone of having my first child. I had watched her give so much love, care, support, and influence to my nieces and cousins, and finally it was my turn to have her be a part of my child's life.

"How could this be? What happened? Who is responsible? I want answers. If I was not in this hospital, I would get to the bottom of what is going on. This should not have happened. I have to see her," I said out loud.

The hospital allowed me to use one of their pumps so that I could leave milk for Eden while I paid respects to my mom. Before we arrived at the hospital the grievous wailing calls from Alabama began to flood my phone.

"What happened?" the relatives all asked.

After being released from the hospital and arranging a memorial service for my mom, I was determined to get answers. I gathered all of her medical records and dug deeply into the events that happened on the day of her passing. I wanted someone to be held responsible for her death. I even spoke with attorneys to see if someone had a legal responsibility for her death.

For about six months, I was enraged. My body had begun to respond to my anger and it spilled over in my character. It was like walking around with rocks in my shoes. Somewhere between six months and a year later it hit me: "Let her go! Accept it and move on."

So, I did.

At least I thought I did.

Yes. There is more.

When Edward Jr. was born, our family was complete. We were living life and doing it well.

My daughter absolutely adored her father and she was the apple of his eye. At the tender age of four, she had already attended three daddy/daughter dances. Each was the highlight of her year. That cliché about daddies and daughters are true. Eden and her father had an inseparable bond. She was truly the apple of his eye and he was her hero. She knew he loved, provided, and protected her.

The matching cliché about mothers and sons also is true. The sweetness, adoration, and affection a son has for his mother is undeniable. I would often declare, "Now *I* have a baby, too."

We had a great family dynamic. We enjoyed life and were beginning to see the fruits of our labors. Financially, we were sound. Our only debt was our mortgage.

About 10 months after my mom's death, I felt the need to face my fears, live out loud, and honor my mom and grandmother, both of whom had passed. It became evident to me that I should do the things I have always wanted to do. Learning to swim was one of those things.

I worked with Team In Training to raise money for cancer research and to face and conquer my fear of swimming. That next year, I hit my fundraising goal and completed an Olympic distance triathlon in the Galveston bay. I inspired my soulmate to do the same. He, too, had a fear of swimming in deep waters, but he decided, "I can do this, too."

The next season, my husband signed up to raise money and train for the Iron Man Half-Triathlon. He, too, completed the swim portion, however he didn't make the time cut-off so he wasn't allowed to finish the race. His finish was truly bittersweet. He trained and invested time and dollars for months, only to be told, "This as far as you can go." The next season he made another attempt with the same disappointing result.

One big challenge with the triathlon is that open water swimming is totally different than swimming in a pool. Edward needed more practice swims in a lake if he was going to qualify to complete an entire triathlon.

"Honey, why don't you get a lake pass so you can get more open-water training in?" I suggested.

So that's what he did. He purchased a lifeguard buoy and started training one to two days per week in open water in addition to his pool swims.

On Sunday, August 19, my husband told me that he had dreamed of a relative's passing. He commented that doesn't mean it was that relative and that it could be anyone. The next morning, he rode his bike to work just as he usually did. When he arrived, he sent me a text message, "I made it. Thank you for waking up this morning. I can't make it without you."

Before leaving work that afternoon, he let me know he would be going to the upcoming triathlon lake site to practice since it was nearly time to decide if he would enter the triathlon a third time.

Typically, after open-water practice, we would take the kids to the neighborhood pool for a family swim. We were determined to keep the kids exposed to water so they wouldn't become fearful. We waited for him, but the time grew later and he still hadn't returned home. I eventually went to the lake and found his car parked and his towel neatly folded in the back of the car, but Ed was nowhere to be found.

That was the beginning of the longest 36 hours of my life.

On Tuesday, diving crews searched the swimming area and found nothing. I remember saying, "See, I told you he wasn't there." But on Wednesday morning, August 22, 2012, my husband's five-foot, eight-inch, 164-pound body floated to the surface of the water.

Edward was gone.

It was like driving down a highway on a beautiful sunny day—everyone is happy and laughing and then—WHAM!—out of nowhere, a truck knocks you across the highway. You are discombobulated and disoriented and feeling like, "What just happened?" I felt numb, with the world spinning around me.

How do you recover from something like that? First my mom, and now just four years later, my husband. They were the two people closest to me and the only family I had. I was left with a 4-½-year-old daughter and a 15-month-old son.

Soon, the lights on all my future dreams slowly went out and it was total darkness. The only thing I remember from that first year was sensing other areas of my life dying off. It was truly devastating. I was emotionally wrecked and mentally desolated. I went deeper and deeper into isolation.

I often remember Edward's memorial service. The service was on a Wednesday at noon, and we thought maybe one hundred people would attend. Instead, it was standing-room only, people packed around the walls and over five hundred people attending.

That wasn't the shocking thing; his company brought a couple of busloads of people to the service. Many were vendors from other companies who had flown in to pay their respects.

*Wow! "Who was I married to?* I wondered. I began to ask myself how I will be remembered by others. More importantly, how did I *want* to be remembered—a victim of my circumstances, or living proof that it's a matter of choice?

*"Hope rises like the Phoenix*

*from the ashes of scattered dreams."* —Quozio.

When your world falls apart, you rebuild. I didn't want to *survive*; I wanted to *thrive*. I wanted to live life by design, not by default, and establish legacy for my children. For me, part of rebuilding and establishing a legacy was sharing my story with people. I knew I wasn't the only person who had faced such adversity, and I believed others might benefit from hearing my words. So, I began to tell my story of "Living Beyond Devastation."

Since making that decision, I have spoken at the Freedom Equity Group International Convention and Anderson Financial Service LLC events, both at the Red Rock Casino in Las Vegas, as well as events in the insurance and financial services industries, professional groups, women's groups, schools, churches, and community events.

When I saw how many women faced the same struggle but without the same means that I had, I founded Widows Mansion Foundation (WMF) in 2015, a 501(c)3. WMF's mission is to provide transitional housing and support for widows and widowers.

My current and upcoming projects include a blog, *Naked & unashamed,* a mission outreach that teams with Kings Ransom Foundation, a non-profit public charity, to free women and children from sex trafficking and building homes for the extreme poor, and publishing my book series *Live Beyond Devastation: From Pain to Purpose.*

What I try to do is live life full throttle and intentionally. If you hope to leave behind a positive legacy, that is what you must do.

# Biography

Regina Diann is a highly regarded speaker, financial strategist and legacy advisor working extensively across the United States and Central America with a variety of businesses including Freedom Equity Group, Missions Me, Kings Ransom, Anderson Financial Services LLC, Fidelity & Guaranty, National Life, American General, and many more.

She is on a mission to empower and equip small businesses, families, single women, and widows with the necessary tactical strategies to not only survive but to thrive in today's economy.

Founder of TWG Insurance and Financial Services, Diann is an accredited investor, a licensed producer, author, speaker, and implementation workshop host. Her unique niche in the financial services arena includes living benefits, tax-free income strategies, and legacy planning and implementation.

Her activities include serving as a technical consultant for Anderson Financial Services LLC, private lending, real estate, options trading, missions, traveling, cooking and most of all spending time with those she loves. Her biggest inspiration and driving force are her two children, Eden and Edward Jr.

Born and reared in Montgomery, Alabama, Regina now resides in Mansfield, Texas, with her fiancée, Lee, and her two children.

## Contact Information:

Facebook: Regina Diann
Facebook: Hope Empowers
Instagram: HopeEmpowers_Transforma

# CHAPTER TWENTY-ONE

# Discovering My
# Faith-Filled Mindset

## Nikki Sheppard

I was the kind of person who planned her whole life. At a very young age, I looked at the world around me and began to silently plan my future. By the time I was five, I had it all figured out. I did not miss a step; my journal was my canvas of possibility. When I was in college, I wrote lists in a pink and green floral journal given to me by one of my beautiful sorority sisters of Alpha Kappa Alpha Sorority, Incorporated, and prayer partner, Anita Moore. Anything was possible in my dream journal. *Maybe* was not an option in my dreams.

I planned my life in such great detail, even down to the type of house I wanted, and the number of children and their genders. I wanted to meet my husband in college, and I did. I wanted to write my own love story and I did. I had this crazy faith and unction that even though I was not the perfect person, God was my source and my all and I knew He would give me my heart's desires. Have you ever had something you were believing in and wanting, a desire that you were struggling to obtain? I believed I just had to be clear on what I wanted.

This confidant woman that I was evolving into was a beautiful warrior princess full of faith and hope, but secretly scared, worried, apprehensive, and uncertain at times. With every twist and turn, even the unpredictable ones, inside I knew that in time it would all be okay. If anybody had my back and would see me through every pain, obstacle, trial, detour, mistake, and fear, it would be my Lord and Savior Jesus Christ. I made the choice to follow Him from the moment I learned of His love.

But my warrior princess faith was tested on the day I walked alone into my doctor's office.

"What do you mean *brain tumor*? What do you mean I may not be able to have kids? What do you mean my dream could possibly be over?" I asked.

I wanted to be the girl with the rare story. I wanted to be the one who defeated the odds. But instead of feeling like the girl who had wanted the perfect life, I wanted to faint, fall on the floor, or have a temper tantrum. I couldn't believe there were people who didn't even want children and here I was, yearning and so sad and scared. Did God truly love me enough to grant me my hopes and desires? What if I was a woman who would never conceive? I didn't even want to think about it.

When hoping and anticipating for a brighter end, you must employ some key principals or you just may not make it. Here I was at the age of 25 facing the very thought possibility of not being able to have children *ever* and it saddened me. I remember playing with Barbies on my bedroom floor as a little girl. I was so excited when I received a black Barbie and black Ken to match. I used to pretend to have a family with Barbie and Ken, with the hope of one day writing a story of my own through imagination, journaling, and prayer.

But hearing my doctor's words, all my dreams and hopes passed before me and I felt hopeless and full of fear that my imagined version of the story might not manifest. I cried out to the only God who could save me. *Why me? What have I done wrong?* I made every effort to do things according to my plan and what was perceived as the American Dream. Here I was, newly married, full of hope, and anticipating a bright future, holding the results of my brain scan in my hand.

I felt a blow in my belly as if I would never achieve my dream. You see, I had brothers and sisters by different parents, but I wanted all my children to have the same mother and father. I wasn't judging anyone who didn't have that same scenario. I just knew that I wanted things to be a little different for my children than it had been for me.

All of my plans, dreams, and hopes were now at risk and I started thinking of ways to create a Plan B. Don't we do that sometimes? If things do not work out one way, we immediately search for other ways to get the outcome we desire. But what was happening in my life was not a part of the plan and not where I wanted my story or dream to end, so something had to change.

I was worried about how I would tell my family that I might not be able to have kids and that I was dealing with a tumor in my brain. I was devastated, confused, lonely, and afraid. My husband wanted to support me completely; however, it was tough because it wasn't *his* health challenge. It was my body, my pain, my dream, my brain.

I appeared to be healthy and strong, yet I was dealing with a second major health issue. Seven years earlier, when

I was 18 and had just graduated from high school, doctors discovered a fibrocystic tumor in my breast, so I was familiar with fear when it comes to a health crisis. I had walked this path before.

The discovery of the first tumor led to surgery and a breast cancer scare. Fortunately, it turned out to be benign. I wondered if that would be the case again or if it would possibly turn out worse. No, I wasn't going to die, but this prognosis could mean the death of my dreams and the sad reality of failure. Brain surgery? How was that going to work? I cried for days and never thought the tears would stop. Have you ever received a dim prognosis from the doctor?

Health problems must be among the hardest and loneliest times in a person's life. Something is growing in your body and you have no idea of what it is, why it developed, or how it got there, much less how to rid yourself of it, much less the fear of being sick and barren. What a scary time.

I did the only thing I knew to do at such times, and that was to pray and cry out to God and declare His scriptures and promises to be true. So, I did just that. I prayed, I fasted, I cried, I worried, I took medication to shrink the tumor, and I received support and encouragement from my family and friends. I was given a low-dose fertility drug to shrink the tumor and over time, the tumor shrank.

What seemed like only a few days was actually months of taking medicine, going back and forth to the doctor, and scans to measure the tumor at every stage to make sure it was shrinking. I wish I could go back in time and talk to that girl who was worried to death, that young adult who was trying so hard to hold on to her faith, that woman who was in need of a breakthrough. She wouldn't have to cry so many nights, and she wouldn't have to question or doubt. I would tell her, *It is going to be okay. You will receive all you hoped for and more.* I would tell her to be patient and remind her that she is a warrior: *You were built for this and you have enough faith for your dreams to manifest.*

I would give her this prayer to repeat: *Thank you, Lord! Thank you for my unborn baby. Thank you for choosing me to be their mom. Thank you for allowing them to get here safely. Thank you, Lord, for giving me the wisdom, the words to say, giving me the scriptures to believe.*

Even before I had any sign of a pregnancy, I laid hands on my belly, prayed daily, and even brought a onesie for my unborn child. Some in my circle probably thought I was crazy, but I did not care. I knew I wanted to be a mother and I knew it would take faith.

I wish I could tell you that the tumor shrank and I got pregnant instantly. I wish I could say that there were no complications afterward. I wish I could tell you that I never cried about any health scares again. People often think that when your breakthrough comes, there will be no more wars to fight, obstacles to overcome, or problems in need of a breakthrough. Sometimes it feels like it is the ripple effect, but when you apply that warrior faith to every single situation presented in your life, the battle becomes a playground of possibility, guaranteed success, and a platform for you to soar.

Who would have thought that 10 years after praying for a baby, I would be writing about conceiving in my book *Blessed to Conceive*? It is a book about my journey to conceive, the scriptures I stood on, the prayers I prayed, and my victory.

The beauty in my story is that after many months of waiting, I became pregnant with my first child, my son, Michael Derae Sheppard Jr. Two years later, I was pregnant with twins, Anyae Christine and Aniya Cimone. To look at my children and see the beauty of their existence is proof that with faith and unlimited beliefs, combined with a positive mindset, there are many things that can manifest in your life.

All three of my children were born healthy and strong and every day they are the living examples that remind me of how anything is possible to those who wait, believe, trust, and then receive. My children have taught me so much about life, possibility, hope, and how to establish and uphold a faith-filled mindset that is driven to achieve everything I want, deserve, and desire in my life.

Sometimes our children teach us the greatest lessons. When my son was two years old and we were driving home from daycare, he was crying for some McDonald's fries. I made the mistake of promising him we would pick up fries on the thirty- to sixty-minute drive home through Los Angeles traffic. I knew the railroad tracks in Inglewood were my marking point and near the closest McDonald's. I kept thinking, if only my son knew and could see that we were on our way to McDonald's and almost there. I kept affirming for him that mommy had not forgotten about his request and that I was sure to get him what he desired, but he had to wait a little bit.

"I want McDonald's! I want McDonald's!" he continued to cry and scream, repeatedly.

"I know baby," I replied. "Mommy is going to get you McDonald's. Hold on for one more minute—please believe me."

"Why doesn't he believe me?" I thought to myself.

I wanted to cry. Can't he understand that we have gone to this McDonald's before and what I promised him those other times was still true today: I was going to give him what he wanted. Even if his *want* wasn't a *need*, I still wanted to bless him with what he wanted because I love him and want to see him happy.

At that moment, my son could not see past his want. Because he was hungry, he was sure those fries were a need, he didn't have a problem crying and shouting about it to the only person whom he knew would be willing to help.

I believe we have the power and ability to receive those wants that are needs, just as was the case with my son. He knew his breakthrough was coming because he knew I loved him and took care of his desires; however, there was a faith issue because he had some level of doubt that it would happen when he wanted it.

A gentle voice whispered in my mind, "You act like your son."

I thought about it and realized it was true. When I waited for my breakthroughs throughout my life, many times I have screamed, shouted, cried, and pleaded with God to make it happen and happen *now*. I didn't want to walk in forbearance and faith. I believed God loved me and wanted me to win by allowing me to receive the desires of my heart, but I wasn't sure when or how He would do it. Each time, that uncertainty caused me to fear He might not grant this breakthrough like He did the others. I was simply unsure if I was worthy of that love or if He loved me enough. Since I heard the quiet voice that day on the way to McDonald's, many people and experiences have reminded me to keep a faith-filled mindset and believe in the manifestation of my desires.

I want to share some of the wisdom I have obtained throughout my life experiences with you, and I don't want to end this chapter without giving you some coaching tips. This isn't just a story about my life, it's also meant to be a road map for a successful breakthrough so you can obtain all your dreams and desires in life.

It is important to have some steps to consider when keeping a faith mindset to apply to our life challenges.

## FAITH To Discover
## Your Breakthrough Mindset

(Fortitude, Acknowledging Your Inner Voice, Intellect, Total Truth, and Honor)

**Fortitude:** You must be mentally and emotionally strong. Believe in the possibility and consider what happens if it works out, *not* what happens if it doesn't work out. Too many times we don't have the results, yet we plan how to cope with the worst. What helps me is to remind myself of my last victory and to put into place the same thoughts and actions I used to make it through that time.

**Acknowledging Your Inner Voice:** Who are you listening to? What voices are you giving power to? What words are you absorbing as truth?

You must be purposeful in your thought patterns. When we listen to the still voice inside us, that positive cheerleader we all have that speaks positivity to us in every situation, we are reminded and accept that it takes full surrender to faith to achieve what we are desiring. "Faith it till it comes," and get in alignment with the voice that's telling you to win.

**Intellect:** Remember that it has nothing to do with education. Life teaches you lessons, so search for the lesson, identify the problem, find the solution, research the Word, stay around positive people, and surround yourself with people who had a similar problem or issue but received a breakthrough and a win.

**Truth:** What do you believe? What is your foundation? Stand on the truth of success and speak those truths until you know they will happen for you just as you want them to. Be positive, firm, and have forbearance.

**Honor:** Give respect to those in your life who have blessed you and honor yourself by living a life worthy of love, respect, and honor.

Where you are lacking, get the help you need whether that be counseling or specialized trainings.

# Biography

Nicole Sheppard holds a Bachelor's Degree in English and Secondary Education from the University of Northern Colorado and Master's Degrees in School Counseling and Professional Counseling from Amberton University. She has extensive experience as a teacher, school counselor, and counselor in private care.

She was born in Tulsa, Oklahoma, and grew up in several different states while her father served in the U.S. Air Force.

Nicole and her family live in Mansfield, Texas.

She is an active member of Word of Truth Family Church in Arlington, Texas, a member of Alpha Kappa Alpha Sorority, Incorporated, President and Co-creator of Not So Basic Movement, a non-profit founded by her children that provides new and gently used tennis shoes to underprivileged children. She also is Founder of the Voice Conference, which highlights the lives of women and men from all over the world who have found their voice, influence, and purpose in life and who are resilient and successful in overcoming major life challenges.

Nicole's expertise is in individual and group coaching, motivational and transformational speaking, and professional staff and administration coaching.

# Contact Information:

Website: allthingsnikkispeaks.com
Email: Findingyourvoicewithnikki@gmail.com

# CHAPTER TWENTY-TWO

# The "Real" You

## Les Brown

Sometimes it's not about changing to become the person you *want* to be; it's about changing to become the person you *need* to be. There is a whole big, expectant world out there waiting on you to do the things you were destined to do – and the only obstacle in the way is YOU. Personal growth can help you conquer that obstacle, but you must first be a willing participant.

Once you have decided that you are that willing participant, follow these four easy stages of increased awareness to help you begin this journey to a "new you." Let's take a quick look at how 1) self-knowledge, 2) self-approval, 3) self-commitment and 4) self-fulfillment intertwine to help you consciously step into greatness.

First of all, in order to see yourself beyond your current circumstances, you must master **self-knowledge**. Simply ask yourself, "What drives me?" And then pause long enough to hear your response. Try to understand what outside forces – positive or negative – are influencing your answer. Many of us suffer from what I call "unconscious incompetence." That means we don't know that we don't know, which leaves the door wide open for others to tell us what we think we need to know. Therefore, before you can fully wake up and change your life, you must understand the frame of reference from which you view the world. Study yourself, study the forces behind your personal history, and study the people in your life. This will help liberate you to grow beyond your imagination.

The second, and perhaps most crucial, stage of personal growth is **self-approval**. Once you begin to know and understand yourself more completely, then you must accept and love yourself. Self-hatred, self-loathing, guilt and long-standing anger only work to block your growth. Don't direct your energy toward this type of self-destruction. Instead, practice self-love and forgiveness and watch how they carry over into your relationships, your work and the world around you, opening up the possibility for others to love you, too. If you need help in boosting your self-approval, try these steps: 1) focus on your gifts, 2) write down at least five things you like about yourself, 3) think about the people who make you feel special, and 4) recall your moments of triumph.

When you are committed to taking life on, life opens up for you. Only then do you become aware of things that you were not aware of before. That is the essence of **self-commitment**. It's like the expanded consciousness that comes whenever I commit to a diet. Suddenly, everywhere I turn, there is FOOD! Or how about when you buy a new car? Suddenly you notice cars exactly like yours, everywhere you go. Well, likewise, when you make a commitment – when your life awareness is expanded – opportunities previously unseen begin to appear, bringing you to a higher level. In this posture, you are running your life, rather than running *from* life.

The fourth stage of self awareness is **self-fulfillment**. Once you have committed to something and achieved it, you then experience a sense of success and empowerment, otherwise known as fulfillment. Your drive for self-fulfillment should be an unending quest; a continual sequence of testing self-knowledge, fortifying self-approval, renewing self-commitment and striving for new levels of self-fulfillment. Once you have accomplished a goal and reached a level of self-fulfillment, it is then time to go back to the first stage in the cycle.

These four stages create synergy for a conscious awareness of your personal growth. But what about learning to deal with all this from a subconscious standpoint? A very interesting book I have read entitled, "A Whole New Mind," by Daniel H. Pink, explains that the key to success today is in the hands of the individual with a whole different kind of thinking than what our informational age has molded us to. The metaphorically "left brain" capacities that fueled that Information Era, are no longer sufficient. Instead, ""right brain" traits of inventiveness, empathy, joyfulness and meaning – increasingly will determine who flourishes and who flounders." (Pink, 2007)

I highly recommend that, in the midst of your busy schedule, if you haven't done so already, pick up this book and engage yourself to a fresh look at what it takes to excel. As I mentioned before, the only real obstacle in your path to personal growth and a fulfilling life is you. If everything around you is changing and growing – then change and grow. Do it today. Remember, we are all counting on you to step into your greatness!

Now even after making all of these changes what would you say if someone walked up to you and asked, "Who are you?" Would you stutter or hesitate before giving some sort of answer? Would you make up something that sounded impressive, but that you know isn't exactly true? Well, to accurately answer the question of who you are, you must first get in touch with the person who lives and breathes on the inside of you.

When you know and understand who you were made to be, you can begin to tap into the innate power of your own uniqueness. That power allows you the freedom to no longer let life hold you back because of nonsense based on what you've done or not done. It gives you the positive energy to move forward in spite of those things.

You are a unique individual. Think about it, out of 400,000,000 sperm, one was spared to allow you to be here today. Then once you got here, you came with total exclusivity! I know for a fact, as a twin myself, how you can look like someone else, even sound like that person, yet when you consider the total you, there is only one. Wow! Just let that thought sink down in you for a moment.

Now, hopefully that helps you to realize that there is a certain quality on the inside of you that was given to you – and only you – in order to make a difference in this world. Whatever that quality is, it was not intended for you to sit on it, or waste it away. Oh no, it was given to you for a purpose! You cannot, however, learn what that purpose is unless you look inside and see what makes your existence so special.

Don't waste time trying to find "you" in other people. When you compare yourself to others, or try to be like them, you deny yourself – and the universe – the opportunity to be blessed by the gifts and talents that were given only to you. You are destined to achieve great things in *your* own special way; not in the same manner as your friends, relatives, co-workers, colleagues or even mentors. Doing so will only leave you unsatisfied. When you are not satisfied, regret creeps in.

If you don't know this already, let me share a little secret with you: In order to live a good life – a life full of purpose and resolve – you must live it with NO REGRETS!

Most people go through their whole life with a long "would've, could've, should've" list. The truth of the matter is, once you've lived through a day, an hour, or a minute, it's done. You cannot go back. So get over it! Go forward! There's so much more for you to accomplish that you don't have time to live in the past trying to fix things.

Keep in mind, though, that living in the past and reflecting on the past are two totally different things. You *can* look back –

and you should – in order to determine what it was about certain experiences that brought you joy and satisfaction, or grief and despair; what caused you to grow and expand your horizons, or left you stagnant and short-sighted.

Although you cannot relive the past, you can learn much about yourself as a result of having lived it. That requires a lot of honesty with yourself, as well as a willingness to do **whatever it takes** to reach your destiny. Of all the things you can acquire in this life, the most valuable has to be the knowledge of what role you are to play on this earth, for the sake of your destiny.

My favorite book says to *"Lean not on your own understanding, but in all your ways, acknowledge Him and He will direct your paths."* In other words, don't rely solely on your own insight regarding what your role is. There's a Creator who made you and knows you better than you know yourself. Therefore, in everything you do, in every direction you take, recognize and consult with that Creator. That's what it means to look on the inside – not at others.

Now, you will have a real answer when someone asks, "Who are you?" You can assure them that, without a shadow of a doubt, you are not here by accident. You can articulate with unwavering conviction what it is you were put on this earth to do. **Learn to do this and watch the real "you" shine through!**

# Biography

Les Brown is a top Motivational Speaker, Speech Coach, and Best-Selling Author, loving father and grandfather, whose passion is empowering youth and helping them have a larger vision for their lives.

Les Brown's straight-from-the-heart, high-energy, passionate message motivates and engages all audiences to step into their greatness, providing them with the motivation to take the next step toward living their dream. Les Brown's charisma, warmth and sense of humor have impacted many lives.

Les Brown's life itself is a true testament to the power of positive thinking and the infinite human potential. Leslie C. Brown was born on February 17, 1945, in an abandoned building on a floor in Liberty City, a low-income section of Miami, Florida, and adopted at six weeks of age by Mrs. Mamie Brown, a 38 year old single woman, cafeteria cook and domestic worker, who had very little education or financial means, but a very big heart and the desire to care for Les Brown and his twin brother, Wesley Brown. Les Brown calls himself "Mrs. Mamie Brown's Baby Boy" and claims "All that I am and all that I ever hoped to be, I owe to my mother".

Les Brown's determination and persistence searching for ways to help Mamie Brown overcome poverty and his philosophy "do whatever it takes to achieve success" led him to become a distinguished authority on harnessing human potential and success. Les Brown's passion to learn and his hunger to realize greatness in himself and others helped him to achieve greatness in spite of not having formal education or training beyond high school.

"My mission is to get a message out that will help people become uncomfortable with their mediocrity. A lot of people are content with their discontent. I want to be the catalyst that enables them to see themselves having more and achieving more."

Les moved to Detroit and rented an office with an attorney, where he slept on the floor and welcomed his reality stating that he did not even want a blanket or pallet on the cold, hard floor to keep him motivated to strive. In 1986, Les entered the public speaking arena on a full-time basis and formed his own company, Les Brown Enterprises, Inc..

Les Brown rose from a hip-talking morning DJ to broadcast manager; from community activist to community leader; from political commentator to three-term State legislator in Ohio; and from a banquet and nightclub emcee to premier Keynote Speaker for audiences as big as 80,000 people, including Fortune 500 companies and organizations all over the world.

As a caring and dedicated Speech Coach, Les Brown has coached and trained numerous successful young speakers all over the nation.

Les Brown is also the author of the highly acclaimed and successful books, "Live Your Dreams" and "It's Not Over Until You Win", and former host of The Les Brown Show, a nationally syndicated daily television talk show which focused on solutions and not on problems.

# Contact Information:

www.lesbrown.com

 thelesbrown

 @LesBrown77

 @thelesbrown

 LesBrown

 LinkedIn@